Dancing
with Horses

Dancing with Horses

Collected Riding on a Loose Rein

Trusting harmony from the very beginning

KLAUS FERDINAND HEMPFLING

Translated by Kristina McCormack

Trafalgar Square Publishing

Translator's Note

Mr. Hempfling's writing style is simply beautiful – clear, direct, and full of feeling. If any of these qualities is lacking in this English translation, the fault lies entirely with my imperfect skills.

Kristina McCormack   May 3, 2000

© Klaus Ferdinand Hempfling
Published in English in 2001

First published in the United States of America in 2001 by
Trafalgar Square Publishing, North Pomfret, Vermont 05053
Reprinted 2001

Printed in Singapore

The right of Klaus Ferdinand Hempfling to be identified as the author of this work in accordance with the Copyright, Design and Patent Act 1988

ISBN: 1-57076-184-1

Library of Congress Card Number: 00-109878

Akedah School
Klaus Ferdinand Hempfling
P O Box/App.255
E-17820 Banyoles
Girona – España
Tel/fax ++ 34 972 190 390
www.hempfling.com

Typeset by Textype Typesetters, Cambridge
Printed by Kyodo Printing Co (S'pore) Pte Ltd
Designed by Judy Linard

This book contains 479 colour photos: 474 from the author's collection, 1 by G. Boiselle, 3 by T. Micek and 1 by Th. Zimmermann; 3 black and white photos; 37 drawings by Christina Bötzel and 4 drawings by Rahel Schale. The illustration on page 30 is from *The Might and Mystery of the Templar* by Louis Charpentier and is used with the kind permission of Walter-Verlag. The illustration on page 54 is from *Horsemanship* by de la Guérinière (reprint Olms, Hildeshiem 1989).

Instructions for picture sequences. Most of the photo series should be viewed from top left to bottom right as shown:

1	2
3	4
5	6
7	8

Contents

An Accompaniment

He was a noble caballero whose entire life had been devoted to horses. Not only was it said of him that he was a very dignified and humble man, but everyone who saw him ride was enthralled by the performance, and deeply moved by his riding ability.

At the age of 96 years, as he lay on his deathbed, he called for his nephew to come to him so that he might bid him farewell. And so it happened: as the nephew was finally turning away to leave the room he saw, for the first time, tears in his uncle's eyes. The old man reached out again for the younger man's hand and said softly: 'It is such a misfortune that I must die just now'.

'Why?' asked his nephew, tenderly stroking the old man's hand. 'This time comes for every man, and you have had a long, rich, blessed life'.

'Yes', said the old one, 'you are right, but it was only about a week ago that I first realized what it means to truly ride a horse'.

K.F.H.

Birgit is playing in a large paddock with Janosch, a seven-year-old part-bred gelding. The tiniest hand signals are sufficient for effective communication. The most important preparation for the work on a loose rein is understanding the language of the horse – body language. Without lunge line, lead rope or reins we develop a system of communication that also works over long distances.

Using this Book

This book describes and depicts, with many colour photos, very practical exercises to practise with the horse. The basis for the work is communication with the body. We ask you not to begin the individual exercises until you have read the book to the end. That way, with a better understanding and a fuller overview, you will master the assignments more easily and perform them more precisely.

The author on Habón, a twelve-year-old pure Spanish stallion, in passage. In the optimal frame and on a loose rein, the horse displays the same fine, stable balance under a rider as a freely moving horse at liberty. Owing to this precise balance, the horse can move in perfect freedom and, at the same time, can be controlled with minimal body movements.

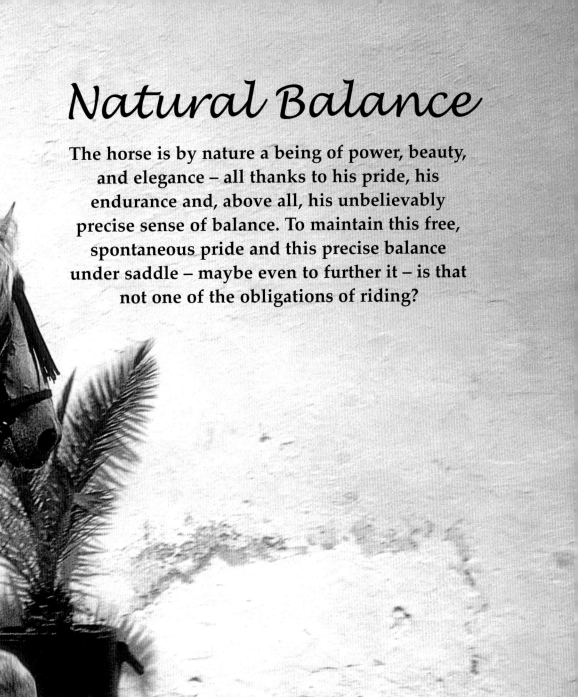

Natural Balance

The horse is by nature a being of power, beauty, and elegance – all thanks to his pride, his endurance and, above all, his unbelievably precise sense of balance. To maintain this free, spontaneous pride and this precise balance under saddle – maybe even to further it – is that not one of the obligations of riding?

Irreconcilable opposites?

It is a fine game that denies gravity –
that game within oneself and in nature
Where the world is without questions,
where life itself is the answer –
where to act is the only law
and experience the reward.

Mankind and the horse have been together for thousands of years. That is a long time in man's view, but only a very short time from the horse's perspective; too short a time, apparently, for the horse to completely adapt to man – to give up his primal nature, his essential wildness, his fierce demand for freedom. And, apparently, too short a time for people to come to an agreement among themselves about the true and correct way to deal with these wild, free creatures. The questions and contradictions surrounding the theme 'horse' which have troubled mankind since the beginning of human thought are as topical, are being asked, defended, and discussed as vehemently today as in the past.

The horse can live quite well without mankind but apparently man cannot live without the horse. Although in many corners of the world today the horse is no longer necessary to survival, nevertheless the number of people wanting to involve themselves with this being is climbing.

But how do you begin?

With all that man has discovered, all that he has accomplished, to this day, the subject of riding, one of the oldest of all, is riddled with endless questions. Moreover, whoever undertakes the study of riding will, on close inspection, be confronted with a multitude of apparent and actual contradictions and paradoxes.

The theme of this book, collected rid-

ing on a loose rein, is one of these paradoxes, and we will examine and discuss others in the following pages.

'Collected riding on a loose rein' – are not those two concepts polar opposites, concepts that cannot even be mentioned together in the same breath? Do not totally different pictures flash through your mind? On the one hand, there are the formally dressed dressage riders with shortened reins on more or less perfectly collected horses and, on the other hand, casually dressed people on horseback streaking across the countryside on long reins, whose mounts are not collected at all. These are, seemingly, people with such opposing riding styles that they can barely examine each other's positions more closely to find some common ground?

How did these 'factions' come to be so certain, so fixed in their positions. Could it be that both sides have part of the truth and can see only this part?

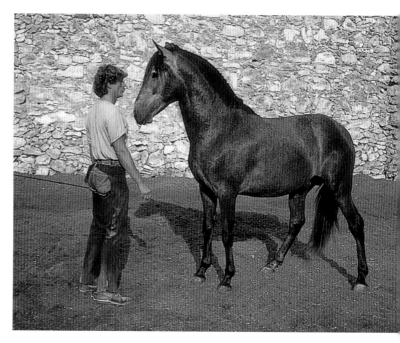

Something brand new?

So many questions, and what now? Now, collected riding on a loose rein!

Is this the reconciliation of opposites? Something brand new? An original and simple solution – Columbus's egg?

At the very least, it is definitely *not* something brand new. It is probably as old as riding itself. Nevertheless, it has managed to stay virtually unknown. Hardly anyone knows what it looks like, hardly anyone has felt it, hardly anyone speaks of it. Why is that? Maybe it is because this has always been something very special, to which only a comparatively small number of people turned, to which only a few could turn. People for whom the horse was far more than just a mode of transportation, or a mere sport, work, or leisure apparatus.

Perhaps this is the reason why the horse occupies such a special place in so many poems, fairy tales, myths, and sagas: the dream of riding, symbolized by the image of the centaur. Is it not a dream of deep bonding, of elemental communication and harmony, a dream of oneness with a being that stands as a symbol of freedom, independence, power and beauty?

The foundation: trust and dominance

The collected horse, a being bursting with pride and power, quiet and yet animated, schooled and strengthened by man solely to carry man upon his back.

Are not the loose reins a symbol of willingness, a symbol of partnership, trust, and harmonious friendship?

In this book I would like to pursue all these things. I would like to pose many questions and, naturally, also to try to answer them. They are all questions about the ways and means for perfect understanding, the common language between horse and human. They are basic questions on the theme of dominance and trust and, last but not least, they are the very fundamental questions about the nature of humanity which are also relevant to our interaction with horses.

And if our work is not about testing ourselves in competition, or wanting to be better than another, or jump higher, then what is the point of it all?

This book is a book of exercises, a practical book, a book to pick up and use, a book that encourages you to participate.

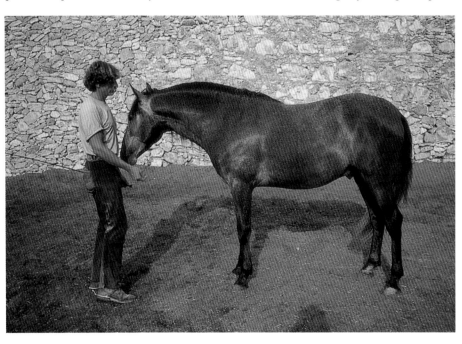

The author with Fulano, a three-year-old pure Spanish stallion. Except for a few days prior to this photo being taken, the horse had lived free in the wilds of the Pyrenees. As usual, I began the free work from the first day on. The work is about building the ideal dominance/trust relationship through specific body signals. During these first encounters the quality of the ensuing horse/human relationship will be decided. This book will cover this topic in detail.

Far away from the bustle of the modern world lives a tradition that has preserved our original access to nature and to the horse.

Below we see one of the last knights of our time, a noble caballero who lives exclusively with and for his horses. 'We ride our horses by the transmission of our thoughts,' say these people, 'an art that has flourished here unchanged through the centuries'.

Step by step I will try to explain why things are meaningful and, I will also make it very clear that riding, in fact the very interaction with horses, can be far, far more than we commonly believe.

Living tradition

In this book we concern ourselves with the practice of making things understandable, demonstrable and, above all, able to be imitated. But behind this practice lives a tradition – right in our own backyard (France, Spain, Portugal and North Africa) – that has preserved and cultivated this very special interaction with horses on which our work is based; invisible to most and far away from the public stadiums, loud spectacles, and vanity fairs.

Why collected riding on a loose rein? What is the purpose of that, other than, it looks incredibly beautiful, it is endlessly light and pleasing, it evidences a pure and wonderful harmony between horse and rider and everything is in perfect balance. Exactly! These words contain a big piece of the whole truth. Perhaps I can

give you a hint of the feeling that is, for me, the pure, true fascination of riding: *el equilibrio natural*, natural balance! Natural balance is the communication between two beings by the most subtle, almost invisible, signals, minute changes in the centre of gravity and **through pure thought and feeling**.

We begin at the very beginning, or, for whom is this book written?

The answer to this is: for every person who in whatever way, shape or form gets involved with horses, regardless of to which riding discipline they feel they belong and regardless of their horse's breed or quality.

Collected riding on a loose rein; it seems a bit like a star, shimmering in the night sky, so very far away, unreachable and other worldly, almost unreal. You see it shimmering and shining and feel a moment of incredible joy at the beauty of this sight and then you turn away, turn back to what is within reach, nearer at hand and more of this world than that tiny light in the night sky.

But let us stay with this example for a moment and allow it to become reality. Jules Verne's *The Trip to the Moon* – also just a dream of mankind's – gave wings to fantasies and dreams and eventually became a reality. The way was incredibly long and demanded enormous effort but, for a handful of people, this dream, to leave our planet and set foot on another heavenly body, came true.

And for the rest of us? The goal was to set foot on the moon but the path to that goal demanded many technological advancements, advancements in transportation and in communication which, today, are useful to all of us and which each of us can use for good or for ill. Only a very few people actually set foot on the moon but their path to the goal brought us all an infinite amount of new knowledge that today is seen as more important and useful than actually reaching the intended goal.

It is exactly the same in the case of our shining star. It is far off and beautiful and even to set off on the journey towards it is an act of great consequence. Many new questions must be asked and many answers must be found, and every answer in itself becomes a rung on the heavenly ladder to the stars.

The young wild stallions, fresh out of the mountains, were driven into a large corral, where they could, over several weeks, accustom themselves to a less free life. After a few days it was possible for me to approach the stallion I had chosen. Because I, one day, want him totally connected to me of his own free will, I place the greatest value on this first contact. I must assume the role of lead stallion in his life but, at the same time, I must win his complete trust. How one accomplishes that, without the use of force, is the subject of this book.

This young stallion was driven into the steer pen; soon the spectacle will begin – his first real confrontation with humans.

The first encounter with the horse

Because the road is so long and the destination so distant, we must be sure that we have prepared especially well. Everything must be very carefully planned. Our equipment must be of the finest quality since it must last for so long and survive much hard use.

Much of this book is, therefore, about just that: the preparation for a long journey. **That is why we place such importance on the beginning, on a secure and stable foundation.** The first encounter with the horse! The first moment so decisive so often repeated, which never loses its significance. Putting on the halter or headcollar, **leading** – it is here that our spaceship is forged, the ship that will catapult us into endless space. Everything must be correct, everything well planned and thought out.

That is why we start at the very bottom. **Nothing is taken for granted.** The typical skills would not take us further in this endeavour anyway. What good is the most perfect car if my desire is to travel to the stars? For that journey I need a vehicle, certainly, but of a totally different type. That is why this book is intended for all people, whether or not they want to reach the stars because, on the journey, there is much to be learned, much knowledge to be gained, something of value for every riding discipline. It is interesting, whether travelling or only dreaming, because the path is the goal.

The path is the goal

This book is filled with picture sequences, practical exercises, detailed instructions, but practice is worthless, or nearly so, without a guiding principle. And, because we are not dealing with postage stamps or motorbikes but with sentient creatures, I must preface the work by exploring this essential point.

Guiding principles seem to have little meaning in a world which knows only goals and where only the winner is important. But what becomes of all the others? Are they to be left by the side of the road? Shall the devil take them? And what about the long, long time between now and the big goal, the ultimate victory? What happens to the days, the years, between now and then? Where do the horses go that could not stay the course? And where do the horses who did make it go after their big win?

This obsession with the goal cannot be a foundation for a journey to the stars, because such a journey is itself marked by constant excitement, living and experiencing fully from second to second, from moment to moment.

All work demands some effort but, it should always be done happily. As I see it, being with horses is a constant joy, free of every frustration. The most important prerequisite for this is: completely setting aside all ambition and, instead, listening and feeling.

Left   Leading a horse correctly is one of the most neglected of skills but in these first steps together a foundation is being built which cannot be made up in any later phase of the work. In this most basic interaction with horses, I can assume the role of lead stallion in a very short time. However, we will come to see that even this most basic skill has many detailed rules.

Right   Trixie is trying, for the first time, to turn and stop her Arabian gelding without the usual apparatus. Here you see the very first steps but already it is a beautiful and elegant picture.

Three truths and the dancing child

Let us compare our journey from dream to reality to that of a small child who wants to dance. He dreams of glamour and glitter but the path to stardom is very long. Perhaps we can all learn something from the experience of this child.

If fortune smiles on him and he finds himself in a good school, with a good teacher, then very soon three essential truths will emerge which are also very important to our work.

1. It is always fun

Admittedly, learning can be hard, very hard, work but the most important thing is that it is always coupled with enjoyment, fulfilment, growth, and progress. In a bad school, our dancing child would be pushed too hard and too fast, for ambition's sake, and very soon he would lose what is most important: his joy and motivation. Eventually only his parents would still hold the dream of the shining star. A good teacher combines play, natural expression and enjoyment when helping a pupil to reach the desired training goal. It is very simple to give this gift to ourselves and to our horses! The most important goal of this book is to illustrate and illuminate this way of working and to make it fully understood that **what we do is only worthwhile if it is done in a spirit of joy and adventure, for ourselves and for our horses**.

My background is in theatre and the arts (for me, the work with horses is the highest form of physical expression and certainly an art) and for a time I had the pleasure of teaching art in a free school in Bochum. The guiding philosophy there was that a child can only really learn if his work is done in a spirit of motivation, insight, and joy. These children were extraordinarily disciplined, and very inde-

Time is, for me, the most important factor in being with horses. Time to listen, time to truly understand the nature of the horse and time to learn from them. Horses are complete and complex beings. How arrogant we are to want to teach them something! No, we can only try to find a way to communicate and then share some moments of this life with one another. However, if we succeed with that, then it is possible to achieve things with horses that are not being accomplished by any 'dressage' in the world.

pendent. The most astounding thing was, however, that no child wanted to go home when classes were finished for the day; they almost had to be thrown out of school. That is what we want to achieve with our horses, that they are so enthralled by the work, so interested in learning and experiencing something new that we must throw them out of the menage at the end of a session.

We will always work so that it is fun for ourselves and our horses – otherwise, what is the point?

2. It is always beautiful

This is a distinguishing feature of our work. When what we are doing is right and good, then it will always look right and good – and beautiful – no matter at which level we are working. If our child, at five or six, at the very beginning of his journey, performs his first tap steps for us, even if it is not an actual dance, does not his performance nevertheless have great charm? Is it not beautiful in its own way, despite its awkwardness?

If the path we follow is a good one, then every single step of training has its own expression, its very own beauty. After all, we are working with beings that symbolize beauty and elegance. We will not say what is so often heard in training stables these days, 'It doesn't look like much now. We need another three years'.

Of course, if I tie up or beat my horse, if I deprive him of his natural way of going, then he will lose all the charm of his natural expression, and, above all, he will stop having fun, he will lose the joy in his work and the sparkle in his eye.

You will find many photographs in this book. Most of them show horses who are just beginning the work, or are still in the very earliest stages. Please decide for yourself whether or not charm, beauty, elegance, strength and joy are already in evidence.

Everything we do will always be beautiful, from the first lesson on.

3. And finally, what happens if . . . ?

What happens if our child never reaches his big goal? If he never becomes a great artist, never achieves mastery? It does not matter. Nothing happens. He had a wonderful time! It was an incredible journey to the stars. And what did he gain (always assuming that he was in a good school with a good teacher)? This person spent all those years developing his own physical presence. He became more confident. He became fit and supple. He discovered and developed his musical talent and his feel for rhythm.

If the path we have embarked upon is good, and we have conquered the need to be bigger and better than everyone else, that is marvellous! Then there is no more stress, everything we do is always fun, is always beautiful and the goal has become irrelevant. It will never be reached, anyway, even by the most talented (*see* An Accompaniment).

So let us begin our journey to the stars, each of us with what he has to offer: come with a perfect astral body, or with your whole assortment of aches and infirmities; with great musical talent or with a tin ear. Let us put ambition to one side and begin to listen and to see. Above all, let us begin to 'feel'! The ability to feel is a gift from God to each of us. Let us begin to feel ourselves and to understand our horses. Let us commit ourselves to this journey which is attended by unending successes and constant joy; this journey that makes it possible for us to stop putting off enjoyment of today's work until tomorrow, or the day after, or until we have achieved some goal of questionable worth. Let us begin this journey that allows us to live fully in the here and now – just as our horses actually teach us to do.

Communication, Dominance and Trust

The horse, in nature, exhibits behaviour characteristics that distinguish it from all other animals. Among these characteristics is the building of a hierarchical social structure yet, within it, the forming of individual friendships. The key to both, to the necessary dominance and to intimate, understanding trust, is horse-based communication – body language.

When we view the whole... the two pillars of riding

This book wants to transmit understanding, not boring grey theory. He who seeks understanding will always try to see the whole picture.

In our western civilization there is a tendency to continually break down the whole into smaller and smaller pieces. So, there are more and more people who know more and more about less and less. The whole – humanity, nature, creation, life – however, falls by the wayside.

In this book we are studying a very primal phenomenon: the interaction of two sentient beings. That is nature, pure nature. If we begin to break this down, pick it apart into small pieces, we risk losing sight of that which is most important.

What, though, is the 'whole', the essence of riding? Very simply, it is **communication and balance**.

The horse has four legs and is incredibly strong. When I swing myself onto his back, there has to be a way to communicate, otherwise, obviously, the whole thing is no fun.

One possible method of communication is, for example, the rude use of whip and rein but, on closer examination, we realize that this is a very primitive, simplistic and, ultimately, not very effective form of communication.

Riding is very simple

If I am somehow successful in communicating with the horse, this primal creature, and we can begin to move off together and are more or less agreed on the general direction, suddenly everything begins to rock, and the beautiful harmony of the horse's movement is lost. He stumbles along, unsure, insecure and experiences me as no great enrichment to his life. So, another problem has arisen – *the equilibrium of shared balance* – but it is no more than that.

Riding, from my point of view, is very simple. I am not just saying that, I mean it. Have you ever noticed how quickly small children learn to ride? Do you know why? Because they do not think on one track as much as adults do. They still use their original body language and are therefore possessed of a basic form of communication. Also, they still have their basic feel for movement and balance. Children show us that everyone can ride because it is one of the most basic and natural things in the world.

With my courses, it is not so much about learning something new but rather about unlearning many things so that you can find your way back to what you once possessed: a basic feeling for your body, a basic form of archetypal communication, the ability to sense and express tempo, rhythm, and balance. It is also about rediscovering and developing your natural self-assurance, self-determination and sense of self-preservation.

Interaction with a horse is one of the most basic of all acts, which is why we must go back to our own basic, original self. It is not all that difficult and, if we do it, things we thought impossible become very possible indeed.

So, let us keep our eye on the whole as we slowly approach our theme and ask ourselves: how can I make myself understood by my horse? What are the possible choices for communicating with him? What assumptions underlie each choice and, above all, when is communication even possible?

It is important for my work that horses understand my signals even at great distances and instantly, trustingly, translate them into action. Gestures of trust and gestures of free, willing submission are repeatedly incorporated into the everyday interplay with one another. These things are very important, particularly with a horse like Janosch because for years he very successfully opposed every human attempt at contact. This horse is not just difficult to school but also difficult to understand. Such horses often end up at the butcher's at a fairly young age and after many changes of owner. If they are approached with understanding, and above all in a horse-oriented manner, then it is just such difficult horses who are the most loyal and willing partners. We will see much more of the difficult, but no less charming, Janosch in this book.

Obey me and love me

In those words is the crux of a basic problem, a basic phenomenon in fact.

We all know that if I beat and punish my horse, he will obey me up to a point, but he will not 'love' me, that is, he will not really trust me and, contrariwise, naturally, it is the same story. What trainer cannot tell a tale of overpetted, spoiled horses, who in gratitude to their doting owners crush them against a wall or caress them tenderly with their hooves?

Trusting or obedient, only one seems possible or, at best, only a little bit of each. **But to work with a horse the way we want to, both trust and obedience are absolutely essential, in their highest form.**

When I began working with horses (and that was not so very long ago) I was told to: 'Smack him around a bit. It is part of the game, part of horse sports'. So I did. Not quite as forcefully as the others, but hard enough to shame myself. I asked myself what right I had to do this. In order that this being would carry me across the countryside or around an arena?

I thought, if someone wanted to give me a dog and told me 'If you want to live with this animal you must hit him ten times every morning', I would certainly say, 'No, thanks', as, I am sure, would you.

Horses do not howl, they just flinch a bit and patiently bear the abuse we mete out. It is their own fault, making it so easy for us!

Maybe I am not hard and manly enough, but I did not want to go on that way. Without much forethought, I bought my first horse, an Arabian mare, and petted her long and lovingly until she nearly broke my upper arm with a powerful blow. That nearly put me off horses but, instead, led to years of study, experimentation, learning and feeling. I explored why a horse behaves as he does and whether it is possible to dominate a horse without punishment, by whatever subtle means. That question is what this book addresses. All the basic exercises have as a goal (among others) the resolution of this paradox.

So, please take me at my word when I write that we never use the whip, or any other instrument (like nose chains, for example) in order to punish a horse. Here in Spain where most of this book evolved, I work daily with young stallions fresh out of the Pyrenees. These animals are wild, powerful, extremely quick and, therefore, not always entirely harmless. After just minutes of work, the ground rules for which I will give you in the following pages, the wild, bucking animal is transformed into a tame horse and the only equipment I need is a simple halter and

24

We are ready. The steer pen is opened and the young stallion shoots out against the lead line. I particularly love this part of the work because it is here that the interaction with the horse is at its most elemental. In Spain a *serrata* (a noseband with a steel chain inlay) is often used. It is a brutal method which I neither employ nor condone. In my work with the young stallions I use merely a stable halter, and there is hardly a more uplifting moment than that split second when the horse turns towards me full of trust. The whole thing lasts only a few minutes. After that we are both bathed in sweat, but those few minutes are formative and decisive. My body language informs the horse that I am a being in whom he can have confidence, to whom he can be submissive, without in the least giving up his pride or his will to live. On the contrary, he says to himself, 'someone who uses so little force to dominate me is someone from whom I can learn comfortably; being with him increases and strengthens my self-confidence'.

This is a very frequently occurring situation on my courses: this Arabian gelding is very frightened but he dominates his owner and is, therefore, quite a difficult horse for her. Although she could saddle him, the process always involved much commotion, a catastrophic situation. How can they be helped?

One option – long hours of 'getting him used to it' – is not only a trying and strenuous experience for all concerned but, above all, an uncertain and, in the end, not very effective method.

I approach the problem from an entirely different point. In just a few minutes I unequivocally clarify the dominance relationship between the two of us. The horse is never tied up in any phase of the work.

If the horse displays unambiguous acceptance of my dominance gestures without in any way humbling himself, and if he shows me his trust throughout so that he follows me everywhere like a small dog (this took two to three minutes), then putting on the blanket is no problem since he trusts me completely. Once the trust is established, there are no more problems because the horse sees that I have no fear of the perceived danger and he, as the lower ranking animal in this relationship, follows my lead.

I do not accustom my horses to plastic bags, rubbish bags, or bright red rubber balls. I accustom them to me. I do exactly what the lead horse in the wild herd does and then no horse will wheel and bolt just because a squirrel decides to sit on the edge of the road. All of this will be discussed in detail in this book.

lead line. Within a few minutes I reach that high level of trust and dominance necessary for our style of riding.

If wild horses are so simple to dominate without whips or chains, it is certainly possible with normal, domesticated horses.

The only 'weapon' we employ is body language, the coordinated sequence of individual movements, absolute awareness and concentration, and a strong will. All of that can be learned and, believe me, our horses help teach us.

Two souls, alas, live in his breast

Let us observe the whole, and proceed in order, step by step. When we observe the behaviour of the herd, preferably a large, wild herd, there are many obvious things that no one really seems to consider. Actually, the way horses behave among themselves is most interesting and much more complex than we generally believe and it is here that we find the secret that lies at the root of the solution to our problem.

In many respects the horse is unique. One very special characteristic makes him a being with whom a singular sort of relationship is necessary; one characteristic, which is as obvious as it is generally unknown. The secret that we want to discover and understand is that the horse exhibits both the behaviour of a herd animal and a 'family' animal. His behaviour, in simple terms, is like a dog's and a cat's at the same time.

We must investigate this more closely and establish why this point is so critically important for our work and, more importantly, for the understanding of the horse's complex psyche.

Dogs, or in their original form, wolves, live together in packs of varying sizes in which the entire social structure is a hier-

archy. This fact is what makes it comparatively easy to train a dog and at the same time have him bond with a person. The loyalty of dogs is legendary, although this behaviour has nothing in common with loyalty in the human sense. That which, in dogs, looks to us like loyalty is in fact an inborn, instinctive drive that compels the dog to subjugate himself to a stronger being and latch on to him for protection. A beaten dog will, whimpering and with his tail between his legs, nevertheless seek to be near his owner, because that owner gives him, within his simple social structure, protection and security. The dog's behaviour in the wild evidences a similar simple linear dominance hierarchy.

He who dominates is loved

Anyone who spends time with dogs is familiar with this phenomenon. After working with a new dog for barely one or two hours, the trainer, up until this first session a stranger to the dog, will be better accepted, and also more loved than the owner (provided, of course, that the trainer is someone who truly understands his craft). The owner is then, understandably,

The horse seeks protection for survival in the large herd, in which the social structure is a dominance hierarchy. If this is observed more closely, though, it will be noticed that very close pair friendships form within the herd. As a rule, these friends are similar in appearance and personality.

jealous and begins to doubt the 'loyalty' of his four-legged friend. But the behaviour of the dog is entirely consistent because whoever knows how to truly dominate him is also 'loved'.

A cat's behaviour, on the other hand, is the exact opposite. Hardly anyone entertains thoughts of training or 'schooling' a cat. You do not win a cat's affection and trust by an ability to dominate it. On the contrary, you approach gently, lovingly and adapt yourself to the cat's wishes. He who shows patience, gentleness and tolerance will be loved by the cat.

The horse, however, lives, as we know, in herds, also of varying sizes. The social structure within a herd is just like that of a wolf pack, hierarchical and very precisely established but if a herd of horses is examined closely, it will be noticed that often two, rarely three, horses will cultivate an especially friendly contact with one another. That is what distinguishes the horse from pure pack or herd animals. **The horse seeks protection in the security of the large herd but has a personal, trusting relationship with, usually, just one companion.** That is the reason you should be careful, when developing a herd, to always increase the number by two.

In this natural behaviour of the horse lies the reason why living with him is both so difficult and so fascinating and it is exactly this behaviour that explains why so many horse owners do not have as good a relationship with their horses as they would like.

The degree of dominance and trust will be evident particularly in critical situations, for example, when a horse spooks when something unexpected happens. It is at this moment that it becomes evident whether or not my horse stays under my control with the most subtle aids. If I am forced to fight him in such a situation, that is, if I need to work harshly with the reins, then all the work that went before was for nothing. Collected riding with a loose rein is not just for the menage but for every situation! Our horses, and we ourselves, do not learn for the riding menage, we learn for life!

A very important stage of schooling the young stallion is just learning to stay near me in any and all circumstances. This is strong evidence of advanced dominance because the mares are just in front of him (out of the picture) calling and tempting. Throughout all this, I never once used any force, not once did I tighten my hold on the lead line. I stand my ground as though I have taken root and show the horse exactly what I want of him. Horses in nature learn exclusively through imitation, and they imitate the one who proves his worth. Precise, clear, unequivocal and dominant bearing, the projecting of your personality, the total renunciation of every angry, enraged reaction, those are the qualities that are acknowledged and command respect in the eyes of a horse, particularly a stallion. We humans have to learn, not the horses!

Weaker or stronger?

A horse is, on the one hand, a herd animal. His multi-million-year-old genetic design compels him to make first and foremost only one very simple decision: to be weak or strong, to dominate or be dominated. There is no middle ground. This assessment can change from one second to the next but the horse always decides on this differentiation first and it is the most important determination in his social behaviour. If a horse is not truly dominated – and we find very few who are – he finds himself in a continual psychic conflict. His genetic imperative compels him to fight, again and again, even if it is only in the form of occasional disobedience. If we are with a horse **it is absolutely essential for his psychic wellbeing that we dominate him completely! Only then can he concern himself with all the secondary questions of life, arrive at a peaceful state of mind, and find his stability and equilibrium**.

The question of dominance is even more decisive for our type of fine, sensitive work, because a horse who resists, even if only occasionally, can never be ridden with the finest, most subtle aids.

As is well known, very simple aids are commonly used in order to clarify the dominance issue at least halfway.

After the questionable use of whip, switch, spur and other such instruments, however, the horse will not creep behind me whimpering as a dog does: he will turn away from me, get lethargic, show anxiety and demonstrate in a wide variety of ways that I am not his friend. My horse will not completely trust me because the other half of his nature is to behave in the elitist, solitary, independent way of an individual or family animal. How do we bring these two natures together? Is it even possible?

The secret of the knights

I shall digress and go back a few centuries in our history to a time when the horse was an incredibly powerful weapon.

In the time between the eleventh and fourteenth centuries, most of western Europe was ruled by a handful of men who called themselves caballeros or knights and who were organized in Christian monastic orders.* They were not only all trained in the art of sword fighting, but they also all had extraordinary horse-handling skills. Ignoring the political and human backdrop to this period and this movement, let us focus for a moment on this extraordinary riding ability and its secret.

In fact, the horsemanship of the knights had such a good reputation that even today, in parts of France and Spain, they speak not of the 'high school' but of 'the monastic school'.

In those times battles were fought mainly on foot with a sword, or on horseback. The Christian knight orders owed their incredible power not least to the perfect control of their horses. What distinguished these men from the masses, who also had horses and who far outnumbered them? It

was something very significant, a secret which they carefully guarded behind the thick walls of their cloisters (and which the orders still guard today). The knights of the orders knew the secret of the two souls of the horse, and they were able to resolve the paradoxes, to reconcile the contradictions. The common folk beat their horses and castrated their stallions in order to be at least partially empowered. So the horses were somewhat obedient but whenever possible, they would desert in the course of duty. Whereas the knights and the caballeros fought against their enemies, the ordinary rider first fought against his horse. The knights rode into battle with horses whose total impulsion and manoeuverability were the result of extremely powerful and collected haunches. They rode into battle with a sword in the right hand and a shield in the left; their horses obeyed simple body signals.

That secret, of which we speak so much here, is grounded in the nature of the horse. Horses are not only strictly hierarchical; among themselves they fight and maintain this structure in a unique way. Let us see what that is.

* Hardly any period of our history is as murky and controversially debated as the age of chivalry, from its beginnings to its presumed passing. Religious, political and other worldly powers fought bitterly for and against one another. Treaties and fronts changed constantly. To this day you wonder who actually fought against whom? We are agreed, though, that the Knights Templar order had a central position of power and organization, and that the discipline of its members and their achievements in many endeavours were far superior to anything comparable at the time. When the discussion here turns to the age of chivalry, I am referring to the transmission of the traditions of this order and to very personal experiences of the teachings of this world, those which have been preserved only by being available by direct access.

With a sword in the right hand and a shield in the left, so the knights rode into battle. Narratives tell us that there were those that rode off to the battlefield without even a bridle, as shown on this fresco from the Templar Chapel at Cressac.

Only the weak fight!

There is something very noteworthy about the dominance behaviour of horses. The status battles of the lower ranking individuals are fought relatively harshly; they kick and bite, competing with each other for spots on the lower levels of the hierarchy.

The higher a horse ascends on the hierarchical ladder, the less rough the methods which are employed to determine his spot or 'fight' his way up become. The highest-ranking horse rarely has to use physical force in order to claim his position. He struts elegantly along and respectfully the path opens before him. The herd needs this animal because the fate of all of them hangs on his instinct, his watchfulness and his experience. Often these top-ranking horses are not even the biggest or the strongest. So how are they singled out? How is their ranking determined and justified?

In the large herds of young stallions, you can study this type of behaviour especially well. Interestingly, the young stallions fight with each other in an almost tender way. Even pecking order conflicts between free rival stallions are compara-

tively harmless, serious injuries are rare. It is not necessarily the stronger horse, the one with physical superiority, who wins. When visible injuries occur in the large stallion herds here on the Spanish *finca* (estate), they stem from ranking battles at the lower end of the hierarchy.

With that fact we are coming closer to the secret of the knights. High-ranking horses have a quality which gives them the power to maintain their position, without constantly having to fight for it. Once a person discovered this secret he would be able to dominate a horse without resorting to any form of physical force. He could caress and dote upon his horse a little in order to win his trust, as he would with a cat and, at the same time, he could dominate him with the same methods that the non-fighting lead stallion uses. This, quite simply, was and is the secret of the caballero, the knight.

High rank through imitation

The knights learned and adopted the behaviour of the highest ranking animals and acquired such a high-ranking position that they could keep it without the use of any physical methods and, at the same time, could also win the complete trust of their horses. They were never rough with their horses in any way. On the contrary, all of their movements were slow, fine, always well meaning, almost dancelike. Their voices were quiet, soft and inspired only trust. Yet, they dominated their horses so completely that the horses responded obediently to the subtlest finest aids imaginable.

If not through gross physical means, how does a top-ranking animal come to dominate and control an entire herd?

The highest-ranking positions are often assumed by horses that are physically inferior to others in the herd. Other qualities count for more and it is these qualities that the horseman should learn and assume, for the benefit of himself and his horse.

The two pillars of dominance

These are two very critical factors.

1. Anyone who has ever encountered a truly dominant stallion or mare is impressed above all by that creature's incredible presence and the force of its personality. There is such power, such dignity, that hardly anyone would dare to question such a being. These components play an exceptionally important role in the animal world: it is not always the big, strong, fast, physically superior animals who direct and lead the others, but rather those who project their presence, magnetism, and will.

Magnetism, presence, dignity, superiority, thoughtfulness, experience, intelligence, these are the qualities that a high-ranking animal must have. These 'weapons' are psychological in nature and far superior to the purely physical 'weapons'.

2. High-ranking animals develop a very specific behaviour repertoire, i.e. a system of signals, by which they can demonstrate and consolidate their power by the most peaceful means. There are very specific behaviour patterns that identify such high-ranking animals. They are almost like genetically programmed 'direction signals'. They are transmitted by movement, gesture – by body language. Actually, they are not so different from the signals that we humans also use, mostly unconsciously.

The horse as medium

The main purpose of this book is to shed light on these two factors, to describe them, and to enable us to use them in our work with horses.

Let us return briefly to our knights. They knew exactly that they could only live, and go to war, with horses who gave them both absolute obedience and absolute trust. They dominated their horses with the power of their personalities, their individual magnetism and with the help of those signals and gestures used exclusively by high-ranking horses in the wild. They cultivated the most humane interaction with their horses that you can imagine, because they took the place of everything, the entire herd, in their horses' lives. They gave their horses a solid dominance structure together with the opportunity for friendship.

All that is the foundation for collected riding on a loose rein. So we have to begin our work at the very beginning, at the time when the rift first developed between our body and our personality. The knights knew this. It was clear to them that only people with a very distinctive, strong presence, a developed personality could interact with horses in the desired way. Accordingly, the process for selecting candidates was extremely difficult. However, the knights also knew that this type of work with horses continually develops and strengthens a person's character. So, interaction with horses was no longer an end in itself but, above all, a means to an end. The horse also served these people in their quest for self-development.

To elaborate further on this all-encompassing and fascinating branch of hippology would take up too much of this book, and must therefore be saved for another. But, to make one last reference to this subject: when, today, in our regimented, technological world, ever more people are being drawn to horses it is not because they see the horse as one more piece of sports equipment, or yet another leisure-time toy, but rather, I am convinced, it is because they intuitively recognize that the horse can show them a pathway into a world to which all other avenues seem to be closed.

Horse language - body language

Every child knows that the horse occasionally twitches his ears and that this means something. However those few signals, which are commonly known, are not nearly sufficient to structure, organize, and keep together a herd of wild horses. In fact the communications system of these creatures among themselves is many times more complicated and diverse than we commonly assume. In order to ride a horse on a loose rein, in order to make yourself understood with the subtle signs and, **above all, in order to gently but truly dominate a horse, it is absolutely necessary to communicate with him**.

We cannot expect a horse to learn our language, although I often have the impression that many riders do expect just that. We, however, are perfectly able to learn the language of the horse in order to create a fantastic basis for understanding one another.

Horses have their own language! It is body language, a language with an unbelievably broad array of possibilities of expression. The lead stallion of a wild herd is usually found at the back of the herd. From that vantage point he can oversee his entire 'area of responsibility' and he communicates with the animals in his herd exclusively through his body language. Specific signals will bring the herd to an abrupt halt and instruct them to stand absolutely still for several minutes. Other signals mean changes of direction and yet others tell the members of the herd to form a circle to defend themselves from a predator.

I am fortunate to be able to work with truly untouched horses who grew up in freedom and thus retain and express their original nature. When visitors interested in my work came here to Spain, I would lead a mare or a young stallion into the picadero and there demonstrate a number of 'little works of art'. The horse would follow me without a lead or lunge line, would make his perfect circles at walk, trot and canter, and allow himself to be brought back into a lower gait or even to a collected halt on the haunches with the subtlest of commands.

Barbara did not have an easy time with her Friesian gelding who, over the years, had taken control in their relationship. So his surprise was that much greater when Barbara suddenly reclaimed the sceptre of power with simple signals. After the reversal of power, however, he was more agreeable than ever before. At last, he had found in Barbara what he had always been seeking, someone who could lead him, someone he could follow.

This was all done in freedom, without any mechanical influence. The horse would work in one direction then change perfectly in order to work in the other direction. After about ten minutes when my short demonstration was over my visitors were quite complimentary about my bit of 'dressage in freedom', although they had surely seen much more spectacular things. The question always came up, 'How much time do you require to train a horse in this manner?' Now came the big surprise when I told them that the horse I had just been working with had only recently come in from the wilds of the Pyrenees, or was in the picadero for the first time today. In fact, this sort of interaction with horses has nothing to do with 'dressage' in the traditional sense, although you could achieve something similar after working for considerably longer with 'dressage training'.

How was this possible? What did I do? The horses of the Pyrenees had had practically no contact with man all their lives. Their world was formed by unspoiled nature and life within the herd. Anything which did not 'speak their language' was strange, menac-

ing, and to be feared. Now a horse and I were standing face to face for perhaps only the second or third time. The horse saw a being with whom he had nothing in common but his reaction was 'This being speaks my language! And he's using symbols that the lead horse has also used. Everything is strange but at least we can understand one another. This creature certainly has a very strange accent but I think that means I'm supposed to follow. And that probably means that there's danger ahead and I should come to a quick stop out of a full gallop . . .'

Gabriele's warmblood mare was originally very difficult and not completely safe. A clear dominance relationship and winning the horse's trust changed everything. With the clear signals of body language, Gabi can come to an understanding with her mare who is working joyfully and with concentration.

Horses are often gruff and rough among themselves but, they never show rage or rancour; these are typically human qualities that have no place in the interaction with a horse. The highest of all feelings is a distinct body signal that, without any emotion, nevertheless clearly transmits the intended message. The horse is given friendly praise, even at his first response, and is sent on as usual.

Humans must learn, not horses

Through the consistent use of horse language, I can not only demonstrate things with a horse that generally can be accomplished only with much more dressage training; the really wonderful thing is that, working in this manner, you can also build a true dominance and trust relationship in a very few minutes. From the first second the horse feels 'understood' in the world of mankind.

Most horses, and probably your horse too, have not grown up in such a natural structure. Because of that, they have most likely had 'bad' experiences of some description with humans. Nevertheless, it is always astounding how quickly even these horses start to communicate with us. In the courses I have given in recent years, most of the participants could work

with their horses as I have described here by the second day. Any 'difficulties' were not on the horse's part, but rather on the human's! The humans had to learn to use their body language in a focussed and conscious way, and to reduce it to the essentials. It is exactly this that I emphasize so strongly in the basic courses – elements that on the surface have so little to do with horses and riding – and yet, it is through these elements that we develop the sensibility, sensitivity and fine feel that – for both the horseman and the horse – later carries over to riding without a problem.

Perfect communication, including the abandonment of all mechanical aids – now the dream of riding is becoming a reality.

Through our kind of horse-oriented work, you become a member of the horse's herd, moreover a high-ranking one. To lead a horse without a lead rope around barrels, and even backward through them, is not dressage or training it is communication. Suddenly, we are no longer ugly two-legged aggressive beings with flat, laid-down ears, we have become beings who, at the very least, speak the same language.

I am doing this exercise with Janosch in a large meadow. The horse can withdraw from the session at any time and run away to graze. I position myself a bit behind the horse and he follows my signal and walks backward through the barrels. This is only possible if both dominance and trust have been established in equal measure. Both will continue to grow in mutual communication.

Here is another typical situation: the horse is afraid. The coloured barrels came in handy for a number of the photographs that you will find in this book but, for Janosch, they were very sinister.

It is easy to accustom a horse to these barrels if I first have his trust, because then he will simply follow me. I talk to him and show him the barrels as I would do with a small child, and look how he responds to my simple hand signal. He overcomes his fear and becomes independent and confident. I cannot tell you often enough how wonderful this type of work with horses is!

I dragged the coloured barrels onto the grass and laid down several poles as well (also coloured). Again, I used distinct body language to slowly lead the horse up to these sinister things. Although he is looking at the barrels with wide eyes and his ears are pricked, he responds to my hand signal and jumps over. Full of pride he comes back to claim the treat he has earned. Once an exercise has worked, I do not repeat it. Now to the poles. Curiosity about what is coming next is clearly written on Janosch's face. A few hand signals and the horse goes through the poles in a zig-zag line totally on his own. Again, this is not dressage. These are exercises that I come up with on the spur of the moment and which the horse performs as the result of our communication (and to help me with the photos).

The ground rules of horse language

You can carry this form of communication over to riding without a problem. A horse learns so quickly to be ridden, to halt and to back up, all without reins. Here again, the prerequisite is precise, clear body language.

Here are the first, most important, rules of communicating with horses.

1. Everything is information – everything!

Just as a deaf person reads lips, so a horse reads the gestures, the carriage and the overall expression of the human body. As a rule, though, we pay so little, or no, attention to our body language, that the gestures and movements we make are contradictory, confusing, and incomprehensible to our horse, so that eventually he gives up all attempts at establishing communication. Our paths diverge and, as a result, we employ more or less harsh physical methods to reach an understanding.

If we truly want to achieve unity with our horses, we must be absolutely aware that every, even the most minuscule, movement of our body, conveys extraordinarily powerful information, whether we are on the horse or on the ground. If we want to communicate with our horses we must first acknowledge that, to them, every expression of our body has content and meaning. Every movement becomes a word, a sentence, a paragraph: information. A person's entire energetic state can be known by and even transferred to the horse. At one of my courses near Munich, I took the time to demonstrate how this happens.

To do this, I chose a mare who needed a little gentling and calming. I exchanged my usual brisk and energetic stride for a slouchy, foot-dragging shuffle. In that manner, I dragged myself along next to this horse, without touching her in any way. I did not tug on the halter or do anything but drag myself along like a zombie next to this horse. After about ten minutes, the horse's owner asked me to stop, because she feared that she would need an ambulance for the mare who had begun dragging herself along just as I was. With a few energetic trot steps, the horse was alert and chipper again, dramatic proof of the **incredible effect our mood and bearing have on the mind and body of the horse**.

If you ever visit a really good Spanish training facility you will see how a Spanish trainer struts along next to his stallions like a rooster preparing to mate and carries himself just as proudly, erect and 'collected' as he would like his horse to be.

This leads to our second rule.

2. Less is more

We have to learn to clearly separate information from idle chatter. It is like having a talkative neighbour: he may have something worthwhile to say to us but it is so deeply buried in chatter and nonsense that we shut off after the second sentence and follow our own train of thought. That is exactly what our horses do. It does not mean they are not concentrating, they are simply overwhelmed by our idle chatter. **To communicate effectively with the body requires the paring of movement and gesture to the barest essentials.**

In all my classes and clinics, this is the part that is the most difficult for the participants. It is absolutely necessary that we sharpen awareness and develop control of the body, of all its movements, so that **the simplest gestures become a language** – a language that is clearly and concisely understood by horses. Usually our bodies are constantly in motion, mostly uncontrolled. Even people who are very reserved in their interaction with other people and rarely resort to using an expressive gesture, are quite often in a state of constant tension which is communicated to horses as gibberish. Video recordings show this very clearly and can be very helpful in developing self-awareness.

This work with horses trains us to become acutely aware of each part of our body. The caballeros do not say, 'I'm going to work with my horse', they say, 'I'm going to meditate with my horse', and this description is actually quite appropriate for our work, which fosters a certain con-

The first encounter with the Andalusian stallion Junque. These photos show that you can influence and regulate the movements of a horse like the conductor of an orchestra. They also show very clearly how attentively the horse observes my movements. In fact, every movement of my body is, for the horse, information that he can translate into action. After several days, this horse will dance precisely to my movements, change direction through the circle, and even show collection in the various gaits. Everything is information!

These photos show me at work with the young stallion, Fulano. To get a young temperamental horse like this to focus on the work, the exercises and the challenges, without tormenting him with gross, mechanical methods, requires a very precise use of your body language. This is the part that most of my seminar participants find the most difficult. Actually, this demands tremendous concentration and discipline from the horseman. See for yourself by standing absolutely still for ten seconds. Do not move at all. Then you will know how long ten seconds can be. When working with horses that is nothing. Often I stand motionless for several minutes in front of an animal – and you have no idea what a potent effect that has.

templative and introspective state, just as Eastern meditation practices do.

With heightened awareness and better concentration we quickly become able to separate what is important from what is not. All our movements become deliberate, fluid, round, graceful, and beautiful. From session to session we discover more clearly the signals and language of our body. We discover and acknowledge how our horses respond to this language – promptly and easily as though led by a spirit hand – and a wonderful understanding and apprecia-

tion of one another begins to evolve.

3. Always use the same 'vocabulary'

Once we begin to work in this way, in accord with the horse's nature, benefits begin to accrue very quickly. Our horses open themselves to us fully and completely, they become very trusting and attached to us. So, it becomes extremely important that we do not confuse these naïve, trusting creatures. Confusion can happen very quickly if we use different vocabulary to elicit one certain response. By 'vocabu-

Once the horse understands that the human too can make himself understandable with his body, then it becomes very important to always work with the same 'vocabulary'. You can see in the top photo (right) that I am slightly dragging my right foot and slowly raising my right arm. That is the signal for the horse to halt.

In the photo beneath that, you see the last step, and then, in the next photo, the horse is standing pretty squarely.

These are not things that we need to teach the horse, these are things that we draw out from his nature. Through precise work and through clear, prescribed 'vocabulary' the movements of horse and man synchronize. The distance between me and the stallion hardly changes at all.

In the second to last photo I am giving another clear signal, to walk. My right arm goes down, the left leg moves forward and the right hip goes back. Immediately the horse begins to move with me. The first steps of a long journey founded on partnership and communication and which adheres to these principles without compromise.

lary', of course, we mean movements, signs, and gestures.

Absolute consistency in our body language is, in practice, much more difficult than it first seems. Horses are often punished for responding exactly and promptly to signals people did not realize they were giving.

This means we must practise constant self-questioning and constant self-control. In the following chapters I will demonstrate and explain the different signals and aids we use. These aids have come directly out of 'horse language'. Each of us will develop our own variations, our unique 'dialect'. That is as it should be. We are unique individuals and the more we immerse ourselves in this type of work with horses, the more we develop our unique essence. It is crucial though, that we remember the specific signs and signals and use them for their specific purposes. If we neglect this rule, our system of communication with our horses might break down.

4. From flow to stimulus

Once again this is something very special and very significant.

Has this ever happened to you? You sit down to watch a television programme, and someone beside you begins to constantly twitch his foot, leg, or little finger – a minimal movement, but eventually it is enough to drive you mad. It is good that it does, because that is exactly what nature wants it to do.

Look at the drawing of a cross section of the human eye on page 44. The dark grey triangle on the left shows the receptors that distinguish colour and the one on the right shows their range (or angle) of vision. The areas bounded by the white triangles (directly adjacent to the dark grey ones) are receptors that distinguish black and white. Those receptors see less clearly but they are much more sensitive.

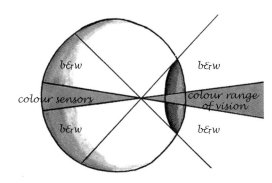

At the outer edge are the motion receptors. These register every single object that moves. Anyone who has ever made a lightening quick leap out of the way of a speeding motorcycle knows how important to survival these receptors are. 'I didn't even see it!' you are likely to say, but nevertheless you responded instantaneously. Because these receptors are so vital to survival, they have top priority in determining our physical response.

If something stimulates these receptors, an automatic reaction will follow, for our own protection, even if our attention is fully engaged elsewhere. That is why a nervous twitching of a finger in the periphery of our vision is so maddening,

our motion receptors are constantly ringing an alarm.

The horse's range of vision is nearly 360 degrees. Most of a horse's eye consists of motion receptors – a very sensible arrangement for a prey animal. Every significant movement in a horse's range of vision is immediately registered and puts him on the alert.

If we are to ride on loose reins with invisible aids, our horse must be able to understand and interpret our slightest, most subtle movements.

Usually, people move without thinking when they are around horses. Their motions are hectic, abrupt and uncontrolled. An untamed horse would panic in such a situation, because his motion receptors would be signaling constant alarms. Our horses, though, have become used to this. They have shut themselves down, become less sensitive, even dull, and therefore they can only be worked with relatively stronger aids. That is exactly what we do not want! Therefore, when we are near horses, we will always move cautiously and slowly. All our movements will be fluid, round, soft, almost dance-

In order to be able to summon a prompt, emphatic reaction from the horse it is important that the signal also be emphatic. From a quiet walking movement came my 'impulsive' stepping under my body, to which the horse responded as pictured.

like. If we twitch our little finger a bit, our horse will respond instantly because he has become sensitized to the tiniest, subtlest prompts.

Everything we do, we do particularly slowly, thoughtfully and quietly. Then, when we, for example, deliberately, but barely perceptibly, cock our hip in a certain way, our horse will recognize that as important information and come to a complete halt out of a full gallop without even the slightest use of the rein.

Communicative riding is unthinkable if we do not observe this basic rule.

5. Softer – softer – now only think it

At the beginning of the work it is important that our prompts are understood as clearly as possible by the horse. So each signal must be given clearly, perhaps even extra clearly. The goal of the work, though, is perfect communication, communication almost by thought alone. To get to that point, it is important to **refine a signal with each repeated use**. This process of refinement can be drawn out over a period of weeks, even months, but the goal of exquisite subtlety will be reached only if this rule is observed from the very first day of the work. And please do not forget that even the finest, subtlest signal must be immediately effective. Even the smallest movement, barely perceptible, can be performed so deliberately, with such clear intent, that it triggers an immediate response.

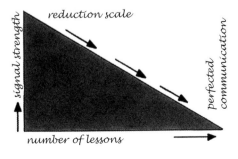

6. Knock before entering

This last rule of our first set is a matter of etiquette. This work with our horses will sensitize them in unexpected ways. When we find ourselves in the harmonious flow of the work, and want to send a new signal (for a change of direction, a transition, etc.) to which we expect an instant response, we should be careful not to 'barge right in', or, as the Germans put it, 'fall into the house with the door'. We should alert our horse to our intention by 'knocking' first. That way, our partner can prepare himself to listen for and respond to our wish. He will not be startled, so he will be able to respond calmly, without tension. In subsequent chapters, I will describe how such 'knocking' can be carried out.

These six rules pertain to our part in this two-way communication, but please do not ever forget that **the horse communicates with us constantly**. He consistently expresses himself and shares with us his opinions and feelings about the work we are doing – both pros and cons. By this, I do not mean extreme behaviour, the obvious cries for help with which we are all familiar.

Let us say, for example, that we are working a horse on a loose lunge line and simply want to reduce the circle. There are a number of very subtle signs and signals by which our equine partner lets us know if we are asking too much, or too little. We must focus not just our eyes but our whole attention on these very subtle signals from our horses. If we do this, we will always have horses who approach their work joyfully, like children who play and, in playing, challenge and discover themselves. **This is not to be confused with lack of discipline;** on the contrary, if we conduct ourselves correctly and with self-discipline, if we are alert, intelligent, mature and open, that is exactly what our horses will reflect back to us. Just as we will rediscover in their behaviour all our own roughness and unjustness.

With the various exercises, again and again I give the horse the opportunity to solve and master the new balance and the centre of gravity changes that arise when I am on his back. Only when we are both successful at this can the horse move naturally and in true harmony with me; only then is riding possible.

Balance
Being Ridden, from the Horse's Point of View

A horse is not born with a saddle. Does even carrying a human cause him damage? In this chapter we would like to examine riding more closely, only not with our eyes, but from the horse's point of view! Not only is this very informative, it also enriches our work.

The best intentions

When we have succeeded in truly communicating with one another – and in the next chapter we will begin that process in a very practical and detailed way – then suddenly the horse 'speaks up', particularly if he is young and green, because we are an inconvenience to him and make him uncomfortable. Balance is not only the rider's problem; it is, especially, a problem for the horse.

My way of interacting with horses and the manner of training and riding are based on certain particular perceptions, acknowledgements and traditions. It is a holistic system and point of view, well founded in its specifics, which encompasses all the components of balance. That means you must take clear, distinct positions in order to make yourself understood and worthy of trust and that you must confront ideas and methods that are neither right nor beautiful but are nevertheless often employed. When we discuss these things we do not do so to criticize or to malign reputations, we do so to further understanding. I assume that everyone has only the best intentions.

The horse is a being of balance and endurance. With his comparatively delicate legs, he can only carry his body mass because he continuously maintains himself in perfect equilibrium. If I, as a rider, now try to adapt this natural 'movement mechanism' to myself, it becomes my responsibility to find the mutual centre of gravity with the horse. If I am successful, then the horse's carriage and head position under a rider will be exactly as they are when he free.

In the beginning was the horse

Left The main principle of my work is never to disturb the horse in his movements. The horse is a creature of nature and, as such, perfect. In his freedom of movement he constantly finds his equilibrium. The task of humans is to help the horse maintain his perfect balance even under a rider; if tautly held lead lines, lunge lines and reins are used then that will never happen. This is Janosch in a fairly early stage of schooling. First he learned to be ridden without reins. That is one of the easiest exercises if people use the natural language of horses. Even in this early stage it can be seen very clearly that a horse undisturbed in his movement and finding the common centre with his rider will discover his natural balance again. Reins are not a help in this, they are, in fact, a hindrance. Inappropriate use of them will actually create exactly the opposite of the lightness, balance and harmony we desire. In comparing the picture (left centre) to the one above, it becomes clear how similar the movements are to each other, with and without a rider.

'Look how beautifully he moves, how he trots, how he canters – isn't that a beautiful sight – just once I'd like it to look like that when I'm riding him!' I often hear this, or similar comments. What is it that so fascinates us in a freely moving horse? It is, I believe, the ease and grace with which this creature moves his fairly large mass. But with this large body mass come comparatively delicate legs. Only because the horse maintains himself in a constant state of balance, is he in a position to move elegantly.

The free horse in nature covers great distances every day but rarely moves quickly, mostly travelling at a walk or slow trot. In play, or in the exuberant bubbling over of good spirits, he will gallop occasionally, but always at a speed that allows him to maintain that very vital balance. Even foals are fascinating in their movements, which from the very beginning are elegant, light, and always in pleasing balance.

Horses are physiologically designed for endurance and balance. They can only cover such long distances every day by continually adapting their movements to

Right Compare the photo right with the one below left. The horse has found his balance under me: he maintains his carriage and his head position automatically, the reins hang loose. I put myself in balance with the horse so that minimal body signals allow me to manoeuver the horse and keep him in collection.

49

The flight response of horses is utilized in horse racing. It can be clearly seen that the balance of the horse has been shifted to burden his forehand. In this situation the haunches are no longer in a position to really carry weight, so they serve only to give a forward push.

the existing circumstances, thereby maintaining their balance. Thus, by moving slowly and in balance they can maintain their energy over a long period of time.

'Look how beautifully he moves!' Why does he not do that under a rider? Can he even do it under a rider?

There are three extraordinary situations in the life of a horse: fight, flight, and being ridden. We shall look at these three things through the eyes of the horse, always from the viewpoint of their impact on balance and endurance. I will try to set out for you how closely these three extraordinary situations are connected with one another.

Flight or fight!

The horse is a prey animal, a flight animal. It is critical for horsemen to know that, in nature, flight, i.e. panic, is practically the only reason the horse gallops very rapidly, so rapidly that out of necessity he works against his two foundation principles, endurance and balance. He expends his energy in a very short period of time and sacrifices his balance by shifting his weight to his forehand. To understand the following we must keep in mind that the flight response is always associated with fear, a surge of adrenaline and panic.

Contrary to this, in a fight response it is not the forehand but the haunches that are burdened. Here impulsion and jumping power can develop, which in fighting situations can mean the difference between victory and defeat.

The big difference

We have established that, in nature, the forehand of the horse is employed to take on an additional burden when the horse is in a state of fear and panic – this is always associated with the negative psychic (and biochemical) components of flight – and the hindquarters are critical in fighting situations, when the ability of an individual to assert his will and exercise his power is at stake. But, if we look objectively at the forehand and haunches of a horse, without making a deep anatomical study of them we will discover one very basic difference.

The **forehand** is built in a relatively linear fashion. Additional burdens on it cannot be relieved through angles and elasticity. On the contrary, any additional stress moves unchecked through this linear system and causes all the well-known injuries.

The **haunches**, on the other hand, are built like an accordion, or similar to a folding ruler. Here resilience and elasticity can be easily developed to accept any additional burdens and, like the shock absorbers in a car, cushion them. Additionally, the haunches come equipped with much greater muscle power than the forehand.

Let us keep these facts in the back of our mind so that we can return to them when we focus our attention on riding.

Left Anyone who works with a number of horses recognizes how often horses tend to fight. The 'togetherness' of horses is marked, above all, by competition and struggle. I am always surprised at how few accidents there are in the horse world since riders are sitting on powder kegs: the honest, good nature of these creatures prevents the worst from happening! It takes only thirty seconds of clear horse language to establish harmony for ever. When fighting, the horse increases the use of his haunches. The power of the haunches determines victory or defeat, in addition to certain psychic factors that are of secondary importance to this point.

Forehand and hindquarters compared

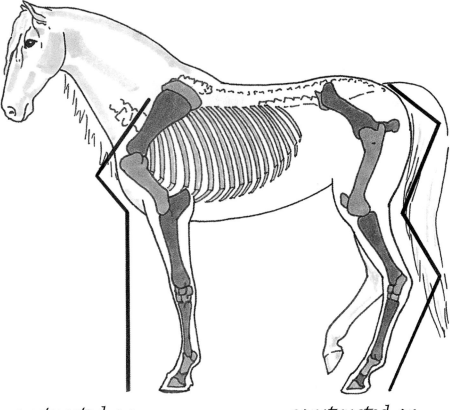

constructed on strictly linear principles

constructed on accordian-like principles

Help, I'm falling!

Before we examine the significance of this section, look at these photos (right). I had asked Britta to sit on my shoulders so that we could play horse and rider. After much commotion, we finally managed it. Once we had found a common centre of gravity, I asked Britta to lean forward. The centre photo shows this moment: a very unstable situation in which we are both in danger of falling flat on our faces. To prevent that, I quickly took a step forward and the situation was saved. What would have happened if Britta continued to lean forward? I would have been forced to take another step forward, and another, and another, faster and faster, with a steadily increasing fear of falling flat on my face.

The circle closes

Why is it that so many riders, and not just the bloodied beginners, complain that their horses occasionally run through their aids and even bolt. The canter becomes faster and faster and nothing can stop the horse. Once he has freed himself of his rider, however, he stands quietly next to him grazing. Now, nothing would make him even think of running away. What really happened here? Exactly what happened to Britta and me; the rider burdened the forehand almost exclusively. That oh-so-important sense of equilibrium was completely lost. When that happens, in order to regain it, the poor horse must put one foot in front of the other, faster and faster, until finally he finds himself in panicked flight and he bolts out of pure fear of falling on his face. Once the 'balance-disturbing-element', the rider, has been eliminated, there is no more fear of falling and no more reason for flight. But what else happened? **The part of the horse**

In the slight blurring the photographer has immortalized Britta's laughter but what the photos make clear is actually a serious and important point. It is a very rocky experience for one person to carry another and is that not also the case for the horse? It is even more problematic when the one on top disturbs the equilibrium. Britta is moving her shoulders slightly forward and thereby forces me to take a step forward so that I do not fall flat on my face. The situation is saved! What would have happened, though, if Britta had stayed in her forward position, is that I would have been forced to take another step forward, and another getting faster and faster. Is that the secret of horses who, having run away, begin peacefully grazing as soon as they have thrown that annoying rider? Does the horse not have the same fear of falling flat on his face as I had carrying a forward-leaning Britta?

that was overburdened by the rider's imbalance is precisely that part that is least equipped to bear it, the forehand: the part of the body which is rigidly and painfully brought into play only when the horse finds himself in panic-stricken flight. The reactions to flight also work in reverse. Just as fear and a surge of adrenaline lead to flight and therefore to the painful loading of the forehand, so the painful loading of the forehand leads, naturally, to fear, and the bodily reactions associated with flight. The vicious circle is complete.

This is the secret that so many 'heavy in the hand' or runaway horses carry within them. This is where the runaway is born, with the 'rider's crutch', the horse's so-called fifth leg, i.e. the constantly taut rein.

Because it is not our intention to compromise anyone's reputation, we departed here from our policy of documenting everything precisely with actual photographs. Original photographs of well-known riders are the basis of the drawings on this page and on the bottom of page 54.

Each of the four drawings shows very clearly, independent of the particular situation, that the major portion of the weight of both rider and horse is pressing on the forehand.

The top illustration shows a phase of canter. The saddle is sitting directly on the forehand, precisely that part of the body unsuited to bear an additional burden. Naturally, the bit must be taken fully in hand to give the horse the feeling, at least psychologically, that he is being supported.

The middle picture illustrates the well-known 'driving seat'. I call it flooring the accelerator with the handbrake on. The action of both rider and horse is played out on the forehand. The haunches can now only perform the forward push; the carrying power of the hindquarters is totally untapped. Rein and forehand carry horse and rider.

We see the same thing with the pair pictured on the bottom who are demonstrating another 'modern' variation of riding without coming any closer to solving the centre of gravity problem.

The pictures on this page and page 55 may illustrate these statements and clarify them. The image of the Spanish bullfighter shows clearly the conformation a horse should have and how he should be ridden so that he can carry the weight of the rider without physical or psychic damage. As mentioned, the possible physical injuries are caused by the horse being ridden on the forehand, but we can see the psychic damage merely by truly looking into the faces of our horses.

Were we to drop a plumb line from above, through the seat of the Spanish rider, we would see that his entire weight is being borne by the horse's powerfully flexed, stepping-under haunches. The horse is in proud carriage and the forehand is free. He is short and compact with his back just long enough to have room for the saddle.

If we use the same plumb line on the 'classical' dressage rider in piaffe, then we realize that even in this 'maximum' collection, the rider is still overburdening the forehand. Her thighs are too far forward to have an influence on the horse's haunches, so their power and energy goes unused. The hoof is barely able to lift above the level of the arena floor.

A rider in piaffe, a collected movement of the High School. A plumb line falling through her body reveals that, even in such a collected exercise, most of the weight is still being carried by the forehand. In comparison, please see the photo of the Spanish bullfighter (right).

Top   In this detail from the Parthenon friezes the horse is small, compact and short backed. It shows all the attributes that we have associated with good riding throughout history. This frieze dates back more than 2000 years. Can 'modern' dressage compete with this?

Middle   The illustration left shows Francois Robichon de la Guérinière in shoulder-in, an exercise about which we will speak extensively in this book. Here too we see the prepared, free, collected horse on a loose rein. When you look at this picture, can you believe that contemporary dressage riding stems from this man and his teachings? No, neither can I!

Bottom   This bullfighter's horse is compact, short backed, and obviously able to carry his rider without damage to himself. The plumb line proves that the under-stepping haunches are strongly and safely carrying the weight of both bodies. The horse is in optimal carriage – the forehand is free and plays.

What does all this mean for us?

A horse does not enter the world with a saddle on his back. If I burden this creature with additional weight, the natural balance comes undone, always to the detriment of the forehand! Riding with a taut rein, which gives the horse his so-called fifth leg, is the consequence.

The lesson to be learned from this is to begin gymnasticizing the horse without the rider's additional weight so that he will be able to carry a rider in balance to a degree. The strengthening of the haunches and back muscles – the initial collection of the horse – begins with the first lesson. Again and again I give the horse exercises which help him to flex the hocks and carry himself and the rider in balance.

In order to ride a horse at all it is absolutely necessary to collect him, that means maintaining his balance under the rider. Maybe this would be a good time to clarify exactly what collection is because, here too, points of view differ greatly.

Cause, effect, illusion: collection and sourdough bread

For thousands of years mankind ate whole grain. It was without question very healthy but it was also very hard to chew and difficult to digest. So, people baked sourdough bread – bread that would last weeks and even months. If you let a simple flour dough stand for a few days then in very particular circumstances certain bacteria form which break down the hard outer covering of the whole grain and convert it into an easily digestible substance. And the great thing is, the bacteria also create gasses which loosen the dough, so that after baking, the bread is soft, easily digested and very tasty.

The cause is that whole grain is practically indigestible without special handling.

The effect is the production of the gasses that make the bread soft and flavourful.

Now comes the deception, **the illusion**.

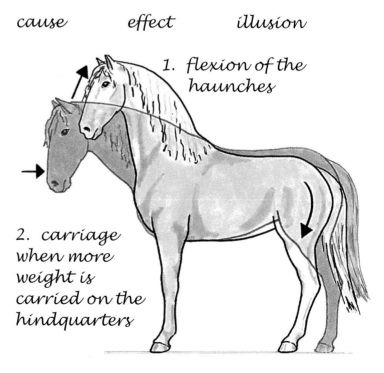

cause   effect   illusion

1. flexion of the haunches

2. carriage when more weight is carried on the hindquarters

3. 'optical frame' without true collection

Today people are once again being drawn to more natural nutrition, to whole-grain products. But, as a rule, the whole grain bread of today has little in common with that of the past and many people who think that it does are living under an unfortunate illusion. It takes quite some time to produce a loaf of sourdough bread. It is much faster to use yeast to make bread. But, the yeast bacteria do not break down the whole grain, they thrive on the milk and honey which must be added to the dough. So, the bread is indeed soft, and also tasty, but indigestible.

The purpose of the 'souring' was not to loosen or to soften the dough but to partially break down the whole grain to make it more digestible. That is why so many people today complain of such a variety of problems connected to the consumption of whole grain products. They have fallen victim to an illusion, tasty though it may be.

Neck up, head on

With collection we also have to deal with cause, effect, and illusion as, sadly, we do in so many areas of our existence. The reason (**cause**) for collection is to gymnasticize and flex the haunches of the horse so that he can accept the weight of the rider and carry it lightly and in balance. The **effect** is that the whole horse comes together, becomes more compact: he gets shorter, carries his neck and head higher and, consequently, more flexed. That, however, is relatively unimportant. What is important is the flexing of the haunches and the shifting of the weight to the hindquarters.

Now comes the yeasty whole grain bread – the **illusion**. To get a horse to work from behind requires much time, patience, and preparation (*see* sourdough bread). However, the external impression (the illusion), the high, flexed head carriage, can be achieved by someone of only moderate skill if he pulls on the reins with sufficient strength. This type of frame and head carriage, so important to many riders, is only indirectly related to collection. If I force the frame and head position through the reins, the horse, in many cases, will drop his back and then flexing the haunches will always be extremely difficult. I do achieve a visual illusion, but my horse is in truth no more prepared to carry my weight than is an indigestible loaf of whole grain yeast bread.

The head carriage and frame are the results of consistent horse-oriented work which enables the horse to 'pull himself together' to carry the rider's weight in balance. The reins are loose, the frame and head carriage are maintained 'automatically'.

High School for the sake of High School?

Definitely not! Please do not forget that all the exercises we see in the dressage arena were originally developed from observations of the movements the horse executed in nature, with the sole purpose of gymnasticizing him and keeping him sound, and there is really no other purpose to High School. The horse is free at the beginning and stays that way to the end. He can carry me in his free natural balance and determine his own way on the constantly loose rein.

Without question, horses schooled in this way would, in certain respects, be judged as deficient or inferior in the usual dressage tests. Not because of the brilliance of their performance, the impulsion, the expression, the power of the movements or the handiness or speed but, rather, because they lacked the precise monotony, the robotlike 'recitation' of a lesson!

My horses are, and stay, free beings! I give my horse the direction and the gait – sometimes not even that – but then I leave him free. Secure and without disturbance he finds his way, unbelievably agile, unbelievably quick. The horse does not notice my weight because I sit in his movement, and put myself in total balance with him. The horse is left to himself and his nature. We go for hours through the country. I have never found anyone who could keep up with me. I have never had a lame or sick horse.

Somewhere in a forest clearing we will play with one another, in shoulder-in, in a half-pass zig-zag, in passage and piaffe. Then, when no one is looking, in the silence of nature and the boundless beauty of solitude, we begin to dance, for our mutual growth and for our mutual pleasure, and, naturally, for the wellbeing of my horse because that is the ultimate purpose.

The Spanish Walk is also a very meaningful High School exercise. Prerequisites are that the horse be in self-carriage, the forehand is free to act, and the hindquarters are stepping under in collection. Even this exercise can be ridden without rein aids. It is not for show, but to develop the sense of play and the expressiveness of the stallion. If the horse is introduced to this movement in the right way, then it is a wonderful method of enhancing his self-confidence.

Big horse, small horse – does size matter?

If you have been following me up to now, you may have already questioned whether all horses are equally suited for this work. In fact, not every horse is suited to being ridden. The breed has hardly anything to do with this but, at the same time, certain breeds, as a rule, produce more good riding horses than others.

The original horse had five sacral vertebrae. In modern sporthorses there are usually seven. That such a longer and normally also taller horse is much more difficult to collect is, I would think, obvious.

Why these horses are bred this way, sadly I do not know, but recently I have begun to detect currents of opinion that would like to see a return to a smaller, squarer conformation. The illustration on page 55 shows a section of the famous Greek Parthenon frieze. The size relationship, of rider to horse, relates to riding in its original form. Since humans were significantly smaller then than they are today, the size of the horses can be estimated at about 13.1 hh. Carrying that equation over to today's man who averages about 5 ft 11 in (1.8 m) tall, would give us a horse size of 14.1 hh at the most.

Many people have written or spoken about the way horses should be evaluated and much of that is very meaningful. I would like to list a few points about judging horses which, as a rule, remain unknown but which are extraordinarily important, both from the viewpoint of natural riding and also from the point of view of the horse.

1. In my experience, a horse intended for a person 5 ft 7 in (1.7 m) tall should measure between 14.1 hh and 15.1 hh.

For a person 5 ft 11 in (1.8 m) tall the horse's height should be between 14.3 hh and 15.3 hh.

2. I think that the first criterion for judging a horse is whether the basic shape of his trunk leans more towards a square or a rectangle. The illustration below clarifies this point. Even a long 'rectangular' horse can be suitable for riding, but considerably more effort is required to prepare him to carry a rider.

square horse
rectangular horse

3. The second criterion is clarified by the illustration on page 60. A basic body structure can be attributed to a horse. I describe horses as either 'concave' or 'convex' depending on their tendency to either shape. A horse is built like a suspension bridge. The forehand and hindquarters are the pillars, the mass in between is, so to speak, suspended.

The human sits on the most sensitive spot, directly between the two pillars. If the body line is more convex, then the horse will not find it difficult to carry a rider, to

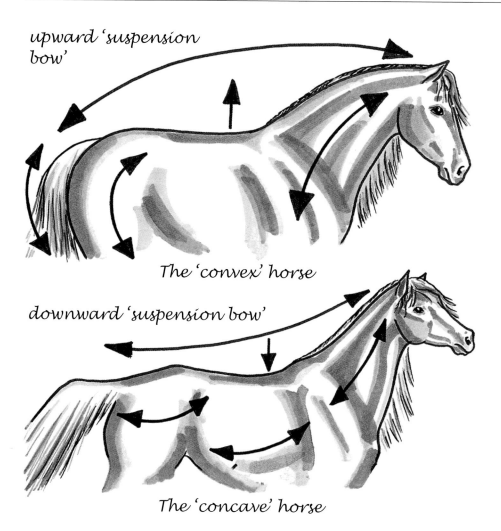

upward 'suspension bow'

The 'convex' horse

downward 'suspension bow'

The 'concave' horse

display collection, and to flex the haunches. If the body line is more concave, then these points are much more difficult for the horse. Unfortunately one very often finds horses of this latter type in the stables of pleasure riders who neglect any and every effort to collect these animals. If only these horses could speak – or cry!

I maintain that the average pleasure rider has neither the knowledge nor the time to train a concave horse to be a riding horse.

4. The width and power of the horse's chest is very important to his balance, the safety of his movements and the longevity of his forelimbs. Today, as a rule, 'fashion' trends determine the appearance of horses, dogs, and proba-

bly also other animals, instead of the appearance being influenced by their natural robustness. Many horses today suffer with chests that are too small, which leads to the forelegs being continually overstressed. Perhaps it looks 'sharp' or 'elegant' but, if the horse winds up at the butcher's as a seven-year-old, this 'visual quality' becomes irrelevant.

5. A decisive point in judging the riding qualities of a horse is the top line in the area of the kidneys. In my opinion, too many horses today suffer from a weak, flat back. Interestingly, that too is, I believe, a question of fashion, because a flat, sunken back seems 'very attractive and harmonious' to many novices.

narrow chest | *powerful chest*

faulty stance | *correct stance*

incorrect loading
of the forehand

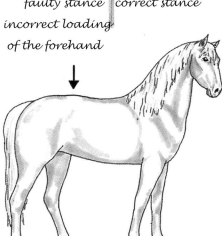

Sadly, a horse with such a back can barely be ridden without pain and what that leads to is a vicious circle: the already sunken back gets pushed down even further. About two hands' width in front of the croup the otherwise harmonious top line of the horse should once again – barely perceptibly to the eye – curve up briefly. The lower illustration above clarifies this point. This trait can be observed in many well-bred Andalusians and also in the hardy, robust breeds. To a novice this trait will most likely look like a negative image since it appears to disrupt the harmonious top line, but then, a novice would not be buying a horse, would he?

6. 'Look at my horse, isn't he a "goer"?' So says the proud horse owner with his newly purchased 'Ferrari'. But, if you glance 'under the hood', (by moving the tail of the horse to one side) you find the motor of a go-cart with barely 15 h.p.

Here in Spain the first thing the *gitanos* (gypsies) do when buying a horse is to move the horse's tail to one side because what use is the most fabulous body if there is no power to put it in gear? To put what determines a good 'engine' on a horse in one book is nearly impossible; your intuition and a person who really knows horses can help you further.

Take the time to study as many horses as possible by 'opening the hood' on each horse (please be careful). The horses whose gaits and appearance truly please you will have a very different musculature between their hind legs, and a very different compactness from those who do not.

There is one last thing to say on this subject: there is no perfect horse but there are horses who 'jump out of the box' and say 'ride me', and there are others who can be made rideable only after very long preparation. A cute poodle with a fuzzy head may be a sweet dog, but you would not want to use him as a watchdog.

If you happen to have a 'sweet, fuzzy headed' horse that does not, perhaps, meet any of our criteria, then keep him and make the best of him that you can. In this book you will find everything that you need to do that but, when you next go to purchase a horse, make it easier for yourself by looking for one that meets the criteria we have mentioned along with all the other commonly known ones.

This is the first time that the young stallion, Fulano, had left the corral where he was driven three days before, and where, for the first time in his life, he had direct contact with humans. After three days of intensive work, our relationship had developed so well that I could safely lead him past the mare herd in a halter and on a loose lead line. Now it is important that the horse consolidates his position and permanently accepts his ranking in relationship to me. To accomplish that we will take many walks together over several weeks, with very specific rules in force. They are the rules of a group of horses in nature.

The Foundation
Leading the Horse

Usually leading a horse serves only to move him from one spot to another. Not infrequently, doubts arise as to who is leading whom! Actually, this simple interaction is one of the most important, foundation-building parts of training. If this phase is simply passed over, then collected riding with subtle aids is virtually impossible. For only in this phase of training can the dominance/trust relationship and the confidence of the horse be built and schooled in the necessary way.

These photos show typical problems that are presented to me at the beginning of my courses. Susanne and Maria have problems with their horses, which make working with them in the desired way impossible. How can a horse understand that he is supposed to respond to subtle aids under saddle when before that he has been constantly pulled around? It is not only *not* beautiful and occasionally quite dangerous, but also a way of interacting with horses that sends them into the worst sort of psychic conflict.

The typical picture?

So it begins!

At the beginning of the course Heide is being pulled across the arena by her Andalusian gelding. The horse dominates, the human is less significant than a mosquito. Communication is not even a topic! This could be changed with chains across the nose and other forceful means but the result would be a withdrawn, maybe obstinate and, above all, fearful and mistrustful animal. Better, faster and more permanent are the laws of the herd and of leading.

To break habits that have been in place for years requires a great deal of energy. The important thing is that the horse is shown his boundaries by body language and correct positioning, not by force.

'The battle over trust and dominance'

On the right road

The next day the picture already looks completely different. The horse is following Heide on a long lead line. The dominance relationship has been resolved with simple means. Not only that, the horse has learned to correctly interpret the hand and body signals. It is understandable that he is not looking totally pleased, since, in the span of a few hours his dominance relationship with his owner has been completely reversed and he has to get used to that.

With Maria and Susanne, too, the picture now looks completely different. Susanne's warmblood gelding adapted to his new, and for him more comfortable, role so quickly that on the second day he was following his partner around without a lead rope. However to begin with, Sam, the Welsh pony, was not happy in a subordinate position.

The Position Circle

I am often confronted – even in my courses and seminars – with very difficult, sometimes even dangerous (made dangerous) animals. As with the young wild stallions, it takes a maximum of several minutes to make a 'gentle as a lamb snuggle bunny' out of a wild horse, or a 'wild' horse. All, naturally, without inflicting any pain on the horse. It is sad that I have had to prove this countless times.

The observers and, above all, the owners of the horses, begin believing in magical powers or some sort of hocus-pocus because, during the entire proceeding, they see more or less nothing!

Naturally, many factors come together in this work. Many of these factors are explained in this book. But, the most important factor of all is knowledge of the 'Position Circle' as I call it. What does that mean? With a horse on a lead rope, you can take a position at any one of the points of the circle shown on page 67. Each point or position has a different meaning. In a very broad way, we can divide the Position Circle into three sections.

The first section (**Zone 1**) is the area of greatest dominance, the most power over the horse. This is the position that a dam takes beside her foal; it is also the position

Zone 1	• **Greatest dominance**
	• **Minimal independence on the horse's part**
	• **Development of the horse's self-responsibility and confident manner is not possible**

Here we can see three different leading positions, which we will describe in more detail. What is important is that all three horsewomen are staying in the first zone of the Position Circle.

that robs the horse of any independence.

Zone 2 marks the positions that subordinate creatures assume. It is the weakest dominance position of all. A person leading a horse, who finds himself in this position, is giving the horse a clear message that he, the human, is the weaker one, the subordinate one. It is noteworthy that this

The position from which most horses are led gives them – mostly unbeknown to the person leading – the most dominance. On pages 73–76 you will see how to lead a horse correctly in observance of the positions described in the Position Circle.

Zone 2	• Least dominance • Development of independence possible within boundaries • Development of the horse's self-responsibility and confident manner possible in boundaries

ZONE 1

ZONE 2   ZONE 2

ZONE 3

position is the one we see used most often.

The positions in **Zone 3** can not only be taken by subordinate animals but also by high-ranking members of the herd. Through the power of his personality, a high-ranking animal or the lead horse maintains relatively great dominance, even from this position.

When we assume this position, after a number of preparatory exercises, we can guide our horse in a way that develops his independence and confidence. We are familiar with this position from long-rein work. This position is the optimum one from which to work a horse in-hand, to guide him, to restrain him, and to challenge him to progress in his work.

In order to assume this position, however, extensive and comprehensive preparatory exercises are absolutely necessary. Please take careful note of this. Later, when we begin work on the High School exercises, the piaffe and passage, this preparatory work is absolutely indispensable.

Zone 3	• Medium dominance • Optimal development of independence • Optimal development of self-responsibility and confidence

The tools we will need to begin

We do not actually need very much to begin our work. Those few things we do need, though, should be functional, and well-fitting where applicable. We need:

1. A 5–6 m (16–20 ft) soft, supple, but nevertheless strong **lead rope**.
2. The finest possible, well-fitting stable **halter**.
3. A long, good quality **whip** which allows a fine, but firm, touch. The quality of the whip plays a role in the success of our work that should not be underestimated. The whip is an extension of my arm and must be employed as gently and precisely as the tips of my fingers. Some very good ones are manufactured in England. **We never use the whip to punish – if we did, it would lose all value for our work.**
4. **The surveyor's-tape lane.** Surveyor's tape is a universal tool for work with horses. Any desired space can be marked off with it to make lanes, corners, etc. The tape lane is approximately 20 m (66 ft) long. It is useful for many exercises.
5. **The picadero.** This is something very special and I will take a little time to describe this 'tool'. The source of this small 'temple of the horse' lies far back in history. You will even find references to it in the Old Testament.

A picadero is basically a small, square menage, or riding arena, with an inner measurement of 10.75 m x 10.75 m (35 ft 4 in x 35 ft 4 in), which means the horses move on a square of 10 m (33 ft) per side. Interestingly enough, this measurement is ideal for horses of all sizes and breeds, from pony to large warmblood. Naturally, it can be just as usefully rigged-up in an open area. The materials we use to define the boundaries of a temporary picadero are virtually irrelevant, it is only impor-

tant that the prescribed measurements be as exact as possible. In such a picadero horses can be trained to High School level.

From Western riders we know of a structure that has a similar function, the so-called round pen. It is, as its name suggests, round, and, as a rule, has a diameter of 10 m (33 ft). I would advise against using it. It does not serve nearly as many purposes as the picadero. The reasons for this are simple. When the Spaniards arrived in America, the idea of the picadero came over with them. Someone had observed that even though the horses

The lead rope we use should be about 5–6 m (16–20 ft) long. It is important that we occasionally are able to keep a great distance from the horse and at no time should the distance between us be too short; the horse always needs the feeling of freedom of free will.

Working in small, bounded areas is very useful. Below we see Gabi leading her mare through the surveyor's-tape lane.

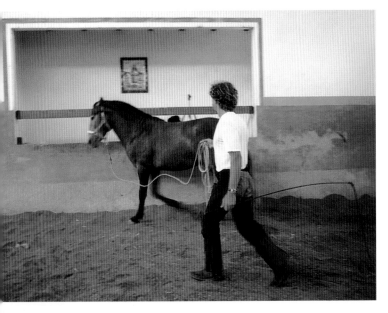

The picadero is a tool of such great importance that it should be constructed, if at all possible, from solid, durable fencing material. Here I am working with Fulano in a typical Spanish picadero. In many cases this structure has the effect of a small temple.

were being worked in a square space they moved in a circle. Once in a while an obstinate horse would hide out in a corner, so the question arose: why not just make it a round space to begin with? At first glance that seems to make sense, but not at second glance. If we look more closely at the 'circle' which horses appear to make in a picadero, then we see that, in truth, it is not an exact circle, but more like a rounded-off square! This figure, which the horse automatically describes, forces him to constantly change his bend so that he is constantly gymnasticizing himself.

We humans, as a rule, live and work in four-cornered rooms. It is a fact that people who stay for an extended time in round rooms lose their orientation and eventually even become ill. It is similar with animals.

The positions taken inside the picadero will vary greatly according to your specific intentions (which we will discuss later). Only that way is it possible to meet the demands of the work in a given moment. This is not possible in a round pen. So, to reiterate, although horses do mostly describe a nearly circular figure inside a picadero, the borders of it should always be square.

6. **The lunge whip** should be comparatively short. I have had great success with many different driving whips.

The olive trees in front of the main building of the finca are exactly 11 m (36 ft) apart, an ideal place to create an improvised outdoor picadero. Many photos in this book were taken in this picadero.

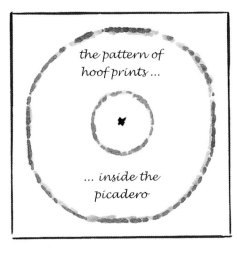

the pattern of hoof prints ...

... inside the picadero

The secret of the halt

Correctly halting a horse is the key point of this whole subject; in that moment during which I succeed in achieving a correct halt, I am able to collect the horse without the mechanical means of the reins. To collect without braking; not a squandering of energy, but rather a transformation of energy. The dance begins!

Every person who has anything to do with horses is familiar with the concept of the full and half halt. But, if people are questioned more precisely about what is meant by those terms and exactly how they execute what is intended, then there has, I feel, always been a dearth of satisfactory answers.

Full halt, half halt: what do the amateurs and professionals say?

The amateurs: full halt – pull back on the reins firmly! Half-halt – pull back on the reins somewhat less firmly!

The professionals (as I understand them): full halt – to bring a horse through into a halt by activating the legs and using the seat to drive a horse into the bridle; half-halt – the horse shortens his stride as he is collected by a diminished use of the above aids.

This is all well and good but, however you understand using the seat and activating the leg aids, it is certain that the reins are necessary, even if, in ideal circumstances, they are not pulled to produce a halt. The seat and leg aids are also employed to 'accelerate' but, if I have understood this correctly, if I leave my reins loose (and 'accelerate' with my seat and leg aids) then my horse will shoot forward. 'Accelerating' and halting or 'braking' are the same aids, only in one case my hand is fixed, and in the other it gives a little, but only a little, because I do not want to give up the collection. If I *have* understood all this correctly, then even among

professionals, the horse is stopped exclusively by the reins, because how the reins are employed is the only difference between accelerating and halting.

And what about pleasure and Western riders? In the end, for most of the reinless-riding pleasure riders, the dream of the loose rein is given up for the short time it takes to halt the horse. Some Western riders can perform perfect stops from a full gallop with truly loose reins. These riders employ their legs, their seat, and the

weight of their upper body which is not brought back but, on the contrary, slightly forward. If it appears that the upper body (of good Western riders) lies a little behind the vertical, it is because the horse steps so far under his body, the haunches flex, and he is in a very pronounced slanted position. Unfortunately, from my point of view, this does not help to train the horse in collection at the higher levels.

Horses running free, without rider and saddle, always stop in balance as they step under with the hind legs. If the lead stallion gives the herd the instruction to halt, then all the horses, like him, halt on the hindquarters. If I use the same command as the lead stallion with my body language, then my horse will stop, without any previous training, perfectly on the hindquarters.

A horse running freely always stops by stepping under with the hindquarters. This action is always connected with his collection. Only by stepping under like this can a horse shorten his stride or slow down without pain. If the rider uses the reins for this purpose then the horse is forced to use the rigid forehand, with all the consequences I have already described. The first thing which the horse, and more importantly the rider, must learn is to shorten the stride, or to halt correctly. This is an essential prerequisite to horse-oriented riding.

Is it possible to carry over this signal of the lead stallion into riding? That would be fantastic, because then I would have the aid I need to halt my horse without the aid of the reins and executed in balance on the haunches! I would also have gained something else that is very important. If I can bring my horse to a collected halt without reins, then it logically follows that I must also be able to develop the half-halt without using the reins, which leads to a shortening of the stride and, thereby, to collection and an upright, high carriage.

The most important building block for collected riding on a loose rein is this kind of collected full and half-halt. By repeatedly practising them in many of the accompanying exercises, we develop the true, genuine flexion of the haunches, genuine collection, without any loss of impulsion.

First, though, let us look at how we can use the work in-hand to bring the horse to the collected halt in accord with the natural way of going.

Full and half-halts from the ground

As mentioned, the horse is above all a long-distance runner, an animal who, thanks to his endurance and constant equilibrium, can move forward over many hours in a quiet tempo. Should the lead stallion give a signal, then what follows is out of the ordinary; the signal succeeds 'impulsively' i.e. it is a momentary interruption of the otherwise uniform flow of movement. The high-ranking animal uses the fact that horses in the wild learn exclusively through imitation and observation and behave accordingly within the group.

For example, certain selected young stallions can actually approach the lead stallion in a way that other high-ranking horses are not permitted to do. The experienced lead stallion will take one such privileged and 'talented' young stallion under his wing in order to train him, 'knowing' that he will one day be defeated by him and perhaps even driven from the herd. Such training happens exclusively through provocation and through learning by imitation: 'do as I do'. This form of imitative behaviour is so rooted in the nature of horses that the lead stallion can bring an entire herd of wild horses to a dead stop with one 'impulsive' halt of his own.

It is difficult to describe how dumbfounded my course participants are when they win control of their horses by such simple means.

Please approach the work without preconceptions and simply try what I describe. If you follow the instructions

The horse in nature learns exclusively through imitation. To stop a horse in this way on a loose lunge line has nothing to do with dressage, it is the natural reflexes which automatically produce this result. Please notice how beautifully this stallion halts on the haunches, how beautiful his carriage and posture are; this is not dressage, but communication.

exactly, you will be surprised by your success.

The signal for a halt from the ground is, in sequence: **out of the flowing movement, 'impulsively' demonstrate to the horse the stepping under of the hindquarters as well as the following deliberate, motionless standing.** This means that the horseman 'jumps' out of flowing movement into a very distinct crouch and **remains momentarily motionless in this stance**.

That last part seems extraordinarily difficult to many people, at least that is my experience with people on my courses. This signal will make practically every horse come to a halt on the spot, on the haunches and in collection.

The signal, which is very pronounced at the beginning, should be reduced and made more subtle each time it is used, until, finally, all it takes is a super-light, barely believable 'twitch' of the hips to bring the horse to a spectacular stop from a full gallop. And the **half-halt**?

To establish the half-halt, use this method to take a horse from trot to walk: as you are walking, bring your hips into a distinct crouch position and continue walking quietly like this for several steps. Once you develop a fine feel for this, the minimal of shifts will then be enough to collect the horse and shorten his stride from the ground without additional aids.

To achieve this is fantastic and when you see how the horses change, how they get rounder, 'shorter', more compact, how, exclusively through this ground work, they gradually come into a cadenced school trot or an expressive, collected canter, you will understand my enthusiasm and you will share it. Every halt that is done in this simple way works on the haunches and the horse stays light and in balance all the time because there is nothing to disturb the harmony of his movements. Later in the book we will discuss the work in the picadero, then when we

In this picture series it can be seen how precisely little Janosch imitates the movement he is shown. He stops with his hindquarters well underneath him. Because of his less-than-perfect conformation, Janosch still brings his head up too far when doing these exercises, but as the work progresses this will correct itself. With each repetition my gesture gets more subtle and still the horse responds promptly and correctly.

come back to these halt and half-halt exercises, you will discover their complex interconnection with the work. But, first, we must go back to the beginning, to practising the leading work and the first halts from the dominant leading position.

The three dominant leading positions

The first leading position gives the horseman the greatest dominance. The torso is turned to face the horse and a stiff whip (to be used by vibrating it) might be used in the early phases for support. The distance between horse and horseman is important and must be respected from the very beginning. Even when the horses are being worked at liberty, the individual leading positions must be held correctly.

Please do not use any aids or equipment for this work other than those which are recommended.

With the exercises and instructions in this chapter, I want to give you a system with which you can, in a very short time, gain great dominance over your horse, to the point where you have his total trust and, at the same time, his complete, joyous, proud and willing submission.

Leading position 1

You are standing facing the horse with your whole body with a distance between you of 1–3 m (3 ft 6 in–10 ft). You should never have less than the minimum distance of 1 m between you! Hold the lead rope with both your right and left hand in such a way that you can spread your arms wide apart. The hand that is near the end of the lead rope (nearest you) also carries a whip, at least for the first two or three sessions. This is only to

The lead rope must always be held so that it loops softly and must never be taut. The horse will learn very quickly to follow willingly at the correct distance from the horseman.

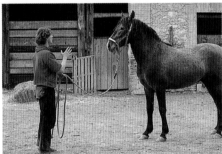

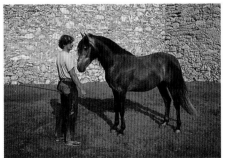

reinforce the body language; **the whip must never be an instrument of punishment**.

Leading position 2

Nothing about the way you hold the lead rope has changed, merely your body positioning relative to the horse. See the photograph above. Here too the distance between you and the horse's head should be no less than 1 m. The 'leading' hand is carried far behind your body, so that it can act as a 'wall' that the horse should accept in a very short time. Please strictly observe this very important point and periodically allow yourself to be watched and corrected by a friend.

Always keep an eye on the horse. Do not just amble mindlessly. That immediately disrupts the fine thread of communication.

These may all seem like very small details but this attention to small, fine nuances creates the foundation, which allows everything that follows to be easily built.

How can a horse learn to react to the finest and subtlest aids, to thoughts alone, if, most of the time, he is being pushed and pulled around? How can a horse be 'directed' without reins if he has not previously learned to respond to the most subtle signs through the work in-hand? A horse is truly dominated when, without any gross aids,

The second leading position is very easily developed from the first. Here the same principles apply as with the first position. We must always take care to keep at least the minimum distance away from the horse and to always keep our eye on him.

Even in critical situations when, for example, (as in the photo on page 75) a stallion is screaming to the mares and shows a desire to race off, it is clear, meaningful body language that counts, not a tight hold on the lead line.

he follows you whenever and wherever you want, freely and joyfully.

Leading position 3

This is the definitive position for leading from the right and left sides of the horse. Again, the way the lead rope is held has not changed. It hangs very loosely. Even in this leading position you should always keep your eyes on the horse and always hold your leading hand behind your body. The horse should walk with his nostrils always in the vicinity of the leading hand! The horse may not overtake the leading hand under any circumstances because then you would find yourself in the second zone of the Position Circle, in exactly that spot where the horseman has the least dominance.

The third leading position is the definitive one in relation to the horse (except for a fourth position which is used only for very specific exercises [see page 190]). It is important that the horseman always moves with his shoulder ahead of the horse's nostrils. If this rule is not observed then the system of communicating by body language collapses.

The photo (left) shows me working the horse from the right. It is most important to work a horse equally from both sides.

As in the photos, left, even when we pause for a while in our work, we should, at least in the early stages, always stay in the correct position.

Working with two people

The schooling of a horse without the help of a kindly friend is possible but only with great difficulty. With exercises up to High School level, many parts of the work should be done with two people.

Working this way not only shortens and makes the long road to a well-trained horse easier, it guarantees a certain control and feedback which you should never do without. I am not talking about the many hours you and your horse will spend with just each other, walking in the country, but purely about the, mostly new, practice sessions.

We begin, very slowly

In the beginning it is easier to study and practise the different phases of the movements with another human. In this photo (right) we see two important phases of leading. Barbara (second from the left) demonstrates the halt. She is taking an energetic step toward her 'horse' and at the same time lifting her leading hand. In the beginning the signals should be extra clear, even a bit exaggerated as our horse must first become accustomed to them, and it is easier for us to differentiate the various signals. To the right of Barbara we see Birgit, lowering her leading hand and cocking back her hip, giving her 'horse' the signal to follow. Please do not forget: if your horse responds in the slightest way, reinforce that with encouraging verbal praise.

Please take a look at the photos below. They tell you more than my words can. Perhaps it seems silly for two adults to be playing horse and rider with one another but it is extraordinarily helpful for the work and will spare the nerves of your horse. Do these exercises with a human friend until all the movements have

become second nature. After all, it is a language which your horse already understands but which you must learn and study.

The principle is very simple. If, when sitting in a car, you want to make something clear to another driver, you do this by using simple and clear hand signals. These movements are not so very different from the ones we want to use with our horses. We also use movements which you may know or recognize from folk and court dances. **Dancing with horses** is not a distant dream, it begins from the first moment of being together and stays with us to the highest levels of riding. **Dancing with horses** means two partners, and each of them has his part, must know his steps, keep his rhythm and develop his grace. **Dancing with horses means first of all learning to dance.**

Let us do the exercises again, but this time with the horse. These exercises may seem laughable to some because they look

Above we see Barbara again, stopping her 'horse' Christiane by taking an energetic step toward her and lifting her leading hand.

The roles are reversed (right). Christiane is now the horse leader; she demonstrates how the leading hand 'predicts' the body language.

The work with the horse becomes much easier and more effective with a human partner. Barbara helps her friend, also Barbara, keep her sometimes self-willed Friesian focussed on the task at hand. Any time the horse's attention turns to something other than the exercise of the moment, Barbara steps into action with light supporting signals. Such help is only absolutely necessary in the first lessons.

so meaningless. I admit that they might but, believe me, they are not easy and, when correctly done, they are effective and fundamental to success.

Your assistant, equipped with a whip **to reinforce the body signals** walks behind the horse. Now, with your body language ask the horse to follow you. It is most likely that he will follow but, if not, **please do not tug on the lead line**. The lead line should always have the same degree of slack. With a small signal from the whip or a simple clucking of the tongue, your assistant will reinforce your command.

Walk directly to the area where you will be working and make sure that the distance between you and your horse does not change. If your horse is day dreaming and does not follow you, your assistant must step into action before the lead line becomes taut.

Most probably, the opposite will be the case: your horse will catch you up, pass you, and maybe even try to run you over, which is exactly what you have to prevent. At the very first sign of the horse demonstrating his power and ignoring you, use your body language in every way possible.

How do you do that? Begin by lifting your hand in a threatening way. No suc-

cess? Then strongly vibrate a whip, which is carried behind you. Still no success? Now begin a 'monkey' dance and keep it up for as long as you need to get your horse's attention. He will be shocked, astounded, confused, or simply laugh himself to death, but he will slow down or even stop. You have won! A small, but very necessary, step on the ladder to dominance. Once your horse has finished laughing, something very important follows: respect.

Once you have arrived at your schooling arena, go around two or three times. Only talk if it is absolutely necessary, keep your eyes on your horse, and walk briskly in a flowing motion, with a proud, powerful stride. Now, if your horse does not respond promptly, your assistant steps carefully into action with supporting gestures.

At intervals, halt your horse two or three times using the body signal we have already discussed, i.e. raise your leading hand slightly and take a clear, distinct, 'impulsive' step toward the horse in an exaggerated crouch position. If you have halted successfully, then remain motionless, do what you expect your horse to do. When you begin to walk off again, please give him a very clear signal.

Ingrid demonstrates, with her pinto gelding, the start of correct leading. While maintaining a constant, consistent distance between herself and her horse, she leads him through the surveyor's-tape lane and stops him with an energetic step directly towards him. She gave the horse verbal signals in advance of the body signals in order not to startle him. After she stops the horse, she remains standing completely still for several moments and then lowers her arm, cocks her hip back, and walks on again.

Finally, quietly lead your horse into his stall or stable in order to end the exercise. The whole thing took only a few minutes but, believe me, the consequences for your relationship with your horse cannot be valued highly enough.

Important It is not the violence of the movements which is important but the aware, 'impulsive', and distinct way they are performed. With minimal gestures, I manage to make myself understood and obeyed by so many stubborn, nervous or wild horses. The decisive thing is your will, your intent, your self-confidence, and the projection of your full presence. All of that is a matter of practice and experience, what is important at first is that you make yourself understood and that you are successful in getting your requests obeyed.

I wish to repeat the following once more because it is truly critical: **at the end of your halt signal, please remain standing as though you are frozen to the spot**. Nothing, not even an eyelid, should move. Count off seven to ten seconds to yourself, silently, and remain motionless during this time. If that turns out to be too long for your horse, which rarely happens, even in the first session, and he begins to walk forward of his own accord, repeat the halt signal and immediately 'freeze' again.

Adhering exactly to these rules is critical to success. You will then see that your horse will stand there as though struck by lightening, and you will also discover how difficult it is to stand absolutely motionless for seven to ten seconds. At the end of this time, move *slowly* into a normal comfortable posture and proceed quietly with the work.

Enough of words! To consolidate and clarify the information given in the text please refer to the pictures.

From signal to praise: give a signal, reinforce it, praise

This is another vital tile in our colourful mosaic.

It is not only important that my horse understands me, it is also important that he takes this information and translates it into action. This should not be taken for granted. If my horse becomes obstinate, it can be due to one of three things: he does not understand, he does not want to understand, or he cannot understand. As a horseman, you must be able to discern the reasons for resistance in order to respond in an appropriate way.

There are two things that, as a rule, my students find very difficult. The first is the true concentration and discipline required to work with horses in this way, and the second is to praise. Since we never resort to the principle of punishment, it is absolutely necessary that we see the positive and constantly reinforce it – that means praise. Praise does not mean that I constantly fawn all over my horse hugging and kissing him. Usually, horses are less fond of that than we believe. No, praise means that, again and again, I give my horse positive feedback during the work, communicative signals that mean I am pleased with what he is doing at the moment.

A short 'good', 'super', 'yes', (or whatever word you prefer) is to a horse like a clearly marked path upon which he can continue peacefully and safely. If for example, I give my horse twenty different signals during a session, I also praise him twenty times, whenever he correctly interprets my intention.

Now to the practical problem. The horse not only has to understand what I mean, he has to translate it into action. That is why I use this mantra: signal, reinforce, praise.

What does that mean? **A signal is always given once only.** I often see busy, dedicated horse lovers on the lungeing circle, giving a command over and over again in a regular pattern. Finally, after the twentieth 'canter' the horse does indeed canter. Probably the signal for canter is given equally often from the saddle. A horse so (un)trained will, naturally, never be able to respond to the subtlest aids because he has learned that after the first signal twenty more will follow so he has plenty of time.

We proceed in an entirely different fashion. A well-trained horse canters on – joyfully, quietly, and powerfully – as soon as the thought is pictured in the rider's mind. Everyone can so sensitize his horse that he responds to the very first soft sign. To do this we must always be absolutely certain that what we are asking of the horse is something he can do easily and joyfully. So we ascend the steps of schooling only to the extent that the desired work can be done **playfully and with enjoyment**.

Praising the horse is vital to our work. Praise does not necessarily mean always hugging and kissing the horse. You can certainly do this generously after the work, as Gabi does here with her sweet mare, but please make certain that your horse actually likes this, because quite a few are less thrilled than their owners about such displays of affection. The praise during the work should be reduced almost exclusively to short vocal signals but these should be given generously and with precise timing.

Let us take a comparatively easy exercise, the transition from walk to trot in the picadero. The sign for the horse, as well as the initial voice command, is lightly lifting the tip of the whip. After just a few minutes every horse will learn to go promptly into the trot as soon as the whip is raised a little. And, needless to say, he will do this without fear of any punishment.

For the horse, these commands are new and unfamiliar so, he probably will not respond at first. Instead of now repeating the verbal command 'trot' we give an enforced signal, for example, a distinct crack of the whip. Now he will begin to trot. When he does, we stop every reinforcement immediately and praise the horse with one or two kind words. At the next attempt you can be sure that a much weaker reinforcement will be sufficient to get the horse to trot and, after three or four minutes, he will be responding to the first small signal.

It is important that the difficulty of the exercises is increased in increments that require only the minimum reinforcements

of the aids and still let us achieve our goal. If we have worked with a horse in this way for some time, the habit of a prompt response will carry over into all subsequent exercises because the horse has learned to immediately interpret an understood signal. If he fails to do this in some future training session, we can be reasonably sure that he has not understood the instruction, the signal.

With regard to **rewarding with treats**, opinions differ on this matter; many trainers are in favour of this, many against. One of the most basic animal instincts is the drive to eat, and, in my opinion, it should be put to good use, but only after there are **no more dominance problems**. If the dominance relationship is not 100 per cent clear, then that annoying, snuffling begging for treats will begin, and that will disrupt the good, concentrated work atmosphere. So, no praising or rewarding with sweet treats in the beginning; once the dominance relationship is clear, in my opinion a timely treat is a wonderful aid.

Correct leading in the dominant position

To continue with the practical leading work. Naturally, you are not expected to keep running backwards ahead of your horse but this position makes it possible for you to have a great deal of control of your horse at the start. After a few practice sessions of being led like this, your horse will probably have realised that, at a certain signal from you, he should follow you, he should keep a certain distance from you which you will establish, and, when you have given him a clear signal, he should halt as well. That is to have learned a lot already.

The photographs on page 82 show you once more the transition from the somewhat uncomfortable first position to the definitive final one. To start, keep the desired distance from your horse and look briefly in the direction of movement, **without totally giving up eye contact with your horse**. Now comes the transition to the final leading position. We also now start to use a medium length lunge whip, or a relatively short driving whip and, at this point, we can dispense with the assistance of our helper and their supporting signals.

Now if our horse does not respond promptly by moving with us, we will give a slight signal reinforcement by twitching the end of the whip. Remember to praise the horse as soon as he responds.

Other important points

- Make sure the horse stays behind you by always keeping your leading hand **behind** your body.
- **Lead your horse from both sides**, changing sides regularly, to ensure that he bends equally well on both sides.
- The kind of leading described here is not meant just to get a horse from one area to another. It is an important phase of training during which the horse learns to comply ever more responsive-

ly to my signals. It also serves to enhance the dominance/trust relationship, and to gymnasticize the horse. If you take your horse for walks, leading in this manner, you can incorporate all sorts of circles and serpentines, thus beginning his suppling.

- A horse that is constantly munching on something, or looking for something to munch, obviously has his thoughts on something other than us. We must curb this habit of eating during our walks from the very beginning and, unfortunately, there is no other way to do it than by – just this once – pulling back sharply on the halter (*see* About punishment and release). There are, however, many situations out in the countryside

The following sequences from my courses help to clarify the exercises. Helmar shows us very nicely how to halt a horse from the second leading position. After only a few more lessons it will be enough for him to merely stand still and the horse will then respond in kind. What is very nice here is the concentrated awareness – the most important quality to bring to work with horses.

Barbara leads the horse from the right. The left arm (the leading hand) is carried behind her and gives the horse a visible boundary. Barbara takes one clear step forward in order to energetically step toward the horse and halt him.

Gabi leads her mare without a lead line. The correctly held whip is always ready to give a signal if the horse lags. The leading position is absolutely correct – horse and horsewoman are very aware of, and focussed on, each other: the start of communication. An energetic step forward, a small turn, and the horse halts.

Here Susanne and her gelding show us what to do if the horse has come too far forward. She simply walks a small volte and when she returns to the hoof prints he is back in the correct position. Clear body language, attentive partners, everything correct.

Here Steffi is in the right position to ask the horse to trot. She gives him a clear signal with her body and supports that with a slight movement of the whip. The horse trots off quietly and is immediately rewarded with a 'well done' from Steffi.

Trixi shows us how to bring a horse from trot to walk without employing a lead line after only a few lessons. She gives a half-halt by stepping more strongly under with her right leg and, at the same time, bringing her left leg along more slowly. Then she proceeds in a quiet walk, and her Arabian gelding follows suit.

in which your horse is permitted to eat and in fact should eat. Sometimes he can eat, sometimes he cannot, and this confuses the horse.

As with treats, there are differences of opinion on how this should be dealt with. I handle this in the following manner, which has proved very useful. Starting on the first walk with a young stallion, I distinctly forbid him to graze but then deliberately go into 'tasty' areas. Then I do nothing more than pull a handful of grass and feed it to the horse. Instantly he understands that he is permitted to eat only after he has been given this signal; a simple but practical and effective method.

83

What happens if the horse always rushes ahead?

Leading, as easy as it may look, is not so simple. To really keep a horse in the desired position when he is being led requires – depending on the type of horse – considerable effort and persistence at the very beginning.

If a horse constantly storms ahead, there are three things to do.

First, it is easy to take the lunge whip from its normal position and move it forward to create a clear boundary.

Second, it is very effective, and very simple, to return to the first, most dominant leading position.

Third, allow the horse to pass you and, in the instant that he does, turn in the

Starting something new is always difficult and things do not always succeed immediately, even for the most attentive horseman. Here we see Trixi who wants to make a volte from a correct leading position but, at the moment, Fox is considerably more interested in a cute mare in the distance. The fine, subtle connection between human and horse has been disrupted. Now, only the lead line can help. What should Trixi have done? That, which must always be done in such situations: react much sooner. In the second photo, it is very clear that Trixi is already aware of the inattentiveness of her horse. At this point, and ideally even earlier, she should have given a small signal with the whip. The horse would certainly have responded and begun working again. If even that had not been successful, it would have been best to stop the exercise and, from a more secure leading position, gently and precisely clarify the situation.

opposite direction (do an about-turn) and begin walking the other way. The horse will follow, and will thereby be back in the lower ranking position again. If you execute this manoeuver now and then, the horse will stay in his position just to avoid all that annoying turning around.

In the end, your horse should follow you everywhere voluntarily. He should walk on when you do; if you slow your pace, so should he; if you go faster, he should go faster too. You are like the boss of a herd to whom your horse orients himself.

Always keep the lead line very long so that your horse can find his own distance from you, that is very important. As a rule, horses are positioned far too close to the humans leading them.

The always-eating horse is an annoyance but not if one adheres to some simple, fundamental schooling principles.

Standing still

Most horses do not stand still either when being groomed or for the farrier. Not only is this a simple, practical exercise for teaching them to stand, but it is also a wonderful tool for strengthening the dominance/trust relationship.

Standing still is a very important exercise for dominance and for discipline. If you have completed the first exercises in this book successfully, then this one should be easy. Our horse has become attentive, he responds to subtle signals, and is able to read our body language. It is critical that, at no time during this exercise do you pass the point at which the invisible bond between human and horse threatens to be broken off. Otherwise, instead of learning 'standing still' the horse will learn 'running away'. Again, this is not training, this is communication.

The photographs on this page show how to halt your horse from the normal leading position. If you work with your horse in this way, he will stand motionless until you give another distinct signal.

If you want to train your horse to stand still when you move away, let the lead rope drop to the ground and distinctly say 'stand'. Naturally, he will not understand that but he has learned to read our signals. So, as you now slowly move away from your horse, hold your palm up in front of your horse and he will remain standing.

There are books and trainers that say that if the horse moves from the spot, then you must always bring him back to it, over and over again until he learns to stand still but this is one thing you should not do. Using this method, you will need forever plus three days to achieve the desired result. I approach it differently, and have great success very quickly.

It is important to begin this exercise only when the horse has mastered leading and halting. When you begin to move away from your horse you must be very observant and you must concentrate because, before your horse actually moves, he will have a slightly annoyed expression ('I'm bored with this'), or he will toss his head, look around, or do something similar. At first, move just a little away from your horse, say 2–3 m (6 ft 6 in–10 ft), and when he shows the first signs of restlessness, respond to those gestures with loud hand clapping. You will be surprised at how well that works. By this stage you should have returned to your horse, before he has had a chance to move from the spot.

If you do that once or twice a day for several days and are successful in anticipating and averting that 'restless' moment, and you reward your horse with a small treat afterwards, he will learn to stand in all circumstances, thanks to positive reinforcement.

Backing a horse from the ground

Once leading, halting and standing still have been mastered, it is good to learn how to back a horse from the ground, that is, how to direct him backwards, not push him backwards, bump him backwards, or cause him to back away from pain.

Again, the subtlest signals and directions must suffice to get the desired response; body language and signals that are almost only thoughts. These must be used from the very beginning because if I begin with gross methods, with yanking, jerking, tugging or dragging, then the standard of communication has been set and subtle work is no longer possible.

We should learn to back a horse from the ground without using any mechanical aids. If we can do that, we have a major, albeit gentle, method of dominance. We do not wave a whip around, manipulate ropes, etc. We never, under any circumstances, employ our bodily strength to direct a horse in any direction

because that will only give our horse direct experience of our bodily weakness.

We will make it a lot easier on ourselves. In the photographs below you will see a very simple arrangement. With simple materials we create a narrow alley, a passageway, into which we lead the horse. Once he is in there, he will have nothing else to do but find his way out again, backwards. We wait for the moment he decides to back out. Occasionally we will help with a few gestures but this is seldom necessary. As soon as the horse begins to reverse – of his own free will – we give a verbal signal, 'back', for example, and take an energetic step toward him to further encourage his backward momentum. Immediately, he gets a treat. **This exercise is not repeated today.**

After we have repeated this exercise once or twice more on subsequent days, then, instead of letting the horse stop backing-up at the end of the passageway, we ask him to move backwards 2–3 m

Even backing up without reins, whether from the ground or under a rider, is not all that difficult if you act in accordance with natural principles. The horse is simply brought into a situation where there is only one way to go, namely backwards. Helmar leads his Trotter into a small alley and supports the horse's independent backing-up with verbal and body signals. Important: never touch the horse with your body during these exercises.

Again, little Janosch must serve as our demonstration horse – but, he enjoys it! The horse is led into a pole alley and is led backwards from the fourth position (*see* page 190). None of this is a problem for the horse. However, if I begin this exercise with pulling, dragging, shoving or commotion, then the horse will always associate it with these unpleasant things and will only perform the movement with pulling, dragging, shoving or commotion.

(6 ft 6 in–10 ft) more, which should be no problem. After this, I begin, step-by-step, to dismantle the passageway and increase the number of backward steps. How quickly you proceed depends on the horse; some horses are already backing easily by the second day. It is important to begin the exercise in the spot where the original alley was set up. Later, you will be able to back your horse anywhere you want.

At the start I said that in backing-up we would acquire a very strong tool for dominance. **Moving backwards is always a gesture of submission for a horse.** In my work with my stallions, I cannot do without this tool. But, we employ it as seldom as possible!

Our goal is to strengthen the self-confidence of our horses each time we work with them. I have just given you the simplest way to back your horse up using simple commands and the force of your personality. Your horse will not be struggling with you and giving you problems with each step. He will be obeying you much more quickly. Backing up is a powerful and serious correction. Please use it knowingly and sparingly because we do not want to oppress our horses, on the contrary, we want them to trust us and be our friends.

One last point on this subject: do not begin backing-up work with horses younger than $2\frac{1}{2}$–3 years old. Beginning any sooner can cause health problems.

Will, mind and the railway worker

Now, at the conclusion of this first section of practice exercises, is the time to illustrate what is, in our work with horses, more important than any technique, any theory. It is the character of a human being, the power of his will, his ability to visualize and, not least, his ability to believe in what he is doing.

'My horse cannot . . . my horse does not . . . my horse will not . . .' But, hardly has someone else been seated on him and suddenly – without force or harsh methods – that same horse can, he does, and he will. There are countless instances of this in my experience.

I want to tell you the tale of the fate of a poor railway worker. His sad end should serve as a lesson for us in many areas of our being, including our work with horses. One Friday, in a small French railway yard a railway employee was working, as he had for so many years. He was working on a refrigeration train whose wagons could be cooled to –30 °C in order to keep the transported wares fresh. On the afternoon of this Friday, a misfortune occurred. Our railway man was inadvertently locked in one of the refrigeration wagons by his colleagues. He spent the whole weekend in his bitter cold prison. On the Monday morning his colleagues found him. He was dead.

So far, this story, though sad, is hardly instructive. However, the point of the story is that the wagon in question, because of a defect, *was not functioning at all*. It was a lovely, sunny weekend and, inside the refrigeration wagon which stood in the blazing sun, it was actually hot. Water and food were readily available but, nevertheless, this man froze to death. His conception of being locked in a refrigeration wagon was enough to create the reality. His *idea*, the power of his mind, killed him.

What we learn from this story is, what a tremendous power our ideas, our conceptions of things, have over us. The laws of reality take a back seat to the power of our minds.

Naturally, that works in both positive and negative ways. If I say to myself three times 'I will not be able to do that' then I will not be able to do whatever 'that' is, even if it is something that I could otherwise accomplish quite easily. However, if I create positive pictures in my imagination then what seemed impossible becomes possible.

That creates an enormous palette of positive and negative possibilities. A small child, who trips two or three times, might be called a clumsy oaf by his father. Okay, the child had something else on his mind besides the bulge in the carpet. However, his father's words are very formative because they create in the boy's mind the idea: 'I'm a klutz, a clumsy oaf'. If it happens a few more times, this boy, perhaps a skilful, talented young lad, will indeed become a clumsy oaf. The father's words became a concept, an idea of the boy's and

There is no element in horse training, or in being with horses, that is as important as the 'psychological foundation'. The best techniques are useless if the state of your mind or the strength of your will are set in opposition.

It is comparatively easy to deceive other people, but horses, never! A horse is a long way ahead of humans in his clarity, his integrity and his honesty, all qualities that we can learn from him.

their effect is as tragic as the idea held by our railway employee.

How should the father deal with his son? In exactly the opposite way. He could simply overlook the boy's tripping. The boy was aware of it himself and would have learned his own lessons from his mistakes. A little later, the child would have mastered the bulge in the carpet and then, if the father wanted to, he could say 'Hey, you did that really well!' By doing that, he would be reinforcing the positive and using it to encourage the boy because, now, the child forms a mental picture that shows him 'Yes! That was very good. I'm actually very skilful'.

We will do just that with our horses. With great foresight we will overlook the errors they make, but we keep our eyes open for the good things they do and praise readily. That way the negative picture fades away from lack of attention, while the positive one is furthered and increased.

If we act this way, every horse is a winner in our eyes because we have disciplined ourselves to see the positive and overlook the rest. The work is marked by a much friendlier energy.

Sadly, each one of us has a collection of negative mental pictures that were formed in childhood. They manifest themselves and have their effect on us, whether we want them to or not. They are mental baggage we carry around with us, each with his own variations, but, it is by no means necessary to continue to reinforce these negative images in our adulthood. Phrases like 'I can't do that', 'it's too hard for me', 'I hope it will work for me', etc., are ones we should totally eliminate from our speech, because they imprint themselves on us and become reality, just as the death of the railway worker became a reality. As adult human beings we must seize our resolve and work consistently to follow our own paths without negative imprinting.

A connection between horse and human that stems from body language and from the power of the mind far overshadows the mechanical connection that depends on rein and lunge line. Building such a powerful connection in the consistent work on the ground is the prerequisite for retaining such communication between rider and horse. The power of the mind is the decisively important thing in any interaction with a horse and, at the same time, every such interaction provides a wonderful opportunity to develop this power.

Thinking – feeling – deciding – doing

Why is that last section in a book on riding? Very simply because self-doubt is picked up by horses from 100 miles away! The horse has no problem submitting himself, but he must trust in the one to whom he submits.

We can deceive ourselves, and we can put one over on our fellow humans by pretending self-confidence and courage where none exist, but this will never work on horses. **Working with a horse means first of all working on oneself.**

'Can I even do that?', 'I do everything wrong', 'Now what did I do?' Do away with all that uncertainty.

Thinking – feeling – deciding – doing. No matter how bad an error, no matter how wrong – everyone makes mistakes! What is important is that we listen to our intuition and do what we believe in – and truly and consistently do just that. If, later, it turns out to be wrong then remember that you did the best you could, knowing what you knew then, but resolve to do better.

Pictures of everyday work

From top left to bottom right

The work with the young stallions demands a great deal of concentration and awareness. Always be decisive in order to be quicker than the horse and to anticipate conflicts *before* they arise.

If the work has progressed far enough, we move our walks from the countryside into town and other lively, active places but, by this time, the dominance/trust relationship must be very well developed.

A typical and critical situation. The horse storms ahead and there is the danger that he will escape from my area of influence. You must react quickly and direct the horse in the opposite direction in order to bring yourself back to the dominant position.

Here it can be seen that the horse selects his own distance from the handler. Always be aware of this. Each horse selects a different and uniquely individual distance.

The lunge whip is important in such situations. Before the horse begins to storm ahead, I can turn his attention back to me by lightly vibrating the whip.

A horse will behave in the company of a good horseman just as he behaves in the herd. Spontaneous rolling is part of that.

Bodily contact, hugging and nuzzling is truly a sweet thing, but always be careful. We must never allow the horse to make the first move of this kind. That affectionate nuzzling and rubbing is

nything but a gesture of
riendship. On the contrary, it
emotes us to a subordinate
pot in the hierarchy, and in
ertain situations it can be a
relude to a real battle.

ven with horses that are
vell ahead with their
chooling, I take the most
lominant first position from
ime to time. I walk back-
vards ahead of the horse but,
leliberately very, very
lowly. The horse is sup-
osed to follow me in the
ame slow tempo. That is an
xtraordinary situation for
he horse, which does not
ccur in nature. In this way I
levelop the horse's concen-
ration and awareness of the
equence of movement. The
orse experiences in a very
lirect and emphatic way
hat he has four legs which
an move in a very
lifferentiated, distinct way.
\fter such a slow-motion
exercise the horse is
enerously praised and
eleased into a free gallop.
\fter one circle around he
vill usually come back of his
own accord to play some
more.

If we are planning to do a new exercise, we do not just barge into the stall and rush the horse to the arena. Instead, we prepare ourselves! We find our inner calm, which is indispensable in our work with horses. We rid ourselves of the tension and stress of the day. We do some gymnastic exer-

cises to loosen and prepare our bodies. We sit for a moment and take some time to imagine the best possible outcome of the exercise. We use the power of our mind, not to freeze to death in the blazing sun, but to survive the freezing cold!

Opaka, the wild mare

Day 1

After the horse, fresh from the mountains, has got a little used to humans and to the halter, she should learn to follow everywhere. I am proceeding exactly as I have instructed you. Alberto always carefully steps in when the horse does not follow promptly. It is important to give clear, precise signals with the leading hand because this will, in the future, be the prelude to the horse's movement. Because the mare has spent more than six years in the wild and has not been spoiled by human hand, she responds promptly and very alertly to all signals. After only a few moments she knows what it is all about and follows me willingly on a loose lead line.

Day 2

On the second day, Alberto's help is no longer necessary. You can clearly see how the mare follows my leading hand with her eye. In a short time, the horse has developed so much trust in me and in my body language that she even follows me into the picadero without hesitating. She is quickly brought onto the track with a few gestures, and even I was surprised at the first halt, which she executed perfectly. Horses that have spent many years in the wild have unbelievably sharpened senses. The slightest signals are sufficient to build communication and an understanding.

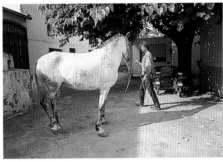

Day 3

On the third day the mare loyally follows me into the picadero without a lead line. With great curiosity she pays attention to every movement of mine and responds immediately. Again and again I praise the horse and speak to her in quiet, gentle words. Our movements take on the quality of a 'love play' and, in fact, this type of work with horses is marked by a deep inner harmony. There must never be anger or rage, the atmosphere is always quiet, peaceful and one of friendly concentration.

The constant praising encouragement is like a road map for the horse, a path upon which she can feel certain and safe. Slowly the doubt leaves her eyes and I direct her to the track.

Day 3

All signals are reinforced by my bearing. Today, too, the mare stops from a light hand signal, nicely on the hindquarters, all without a lunge line. Slowly I come closer to her, this horse who, until a few days ago, had known nothing but the wildness of the mountains. Anxiously she watches my approach, but does not move from the spot. Finally I stroke her withers tenderly before giving her the signal to follow me. I bring my hip backward and lower my hand invitingly. For a brief moment I withdraw my gaze from the eyes of the mare. Hesitantly, but with a friendly, trusting expression she follows my guiding hand. A solid foundation between human and horse has been laid.

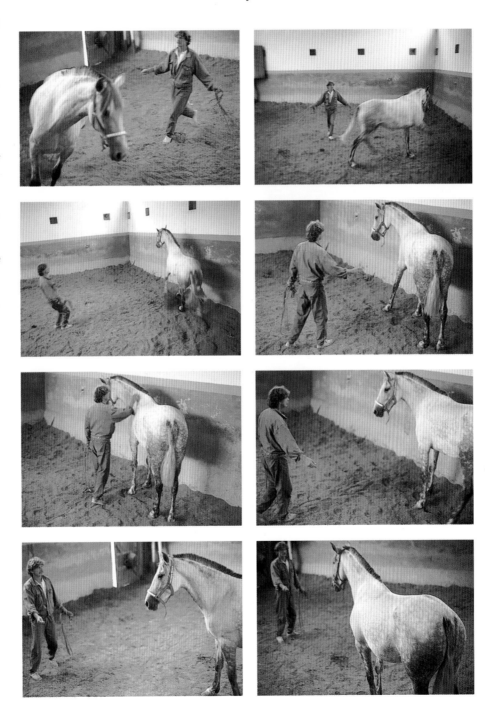

Here I am working with Habón in a small outdoor picadero. Every gesture and every movement is attentively observed by the stallion and appropriately interpreted. Critical to this work, which has nothing to do with lungeing as we know it, is, again, the fact that tasks for the horse are always only suggestions which the horse can then execute in his own way, unfettered and freely. Every type of mechanical 'aid', every instrument of torture, is totally out of place in this fine, sensitive work.

The Picadero
The Circle at Liberty and Lunge Work

The picadero, a small menage (indoor or outdoor) of about 11 m (36 ft) square. With this tool it is possible to bring forth true miracles. Remember this important principle: the lead line and lunge line loop softly – the horse is always free!

Are horses without morals?

Before we begin with the work in the picadero, I would like to describe an experience that occurs frequently.

A woman who had reserved a spot in a forthcoming clinic called me. She was desperate. For several days her mare had done nothing but buck and had undergone a complete personality change. I listened to a brief description of this horse's background in order to propose a tentative diagnosis; I told the woman that she owned a good horse of strong character and that the behaviour she had described was a very frequently encountered phenomenon. Horses behave that way, they rebel, because they want to protect themselves from **total physical ruin**.

A horse has no morality. He does not differentiate between good and evil. Only a human thinks in such categories, and spends his whole life trying to keep these two things even partly separate.

A horse always behaves logically. Unless what happens to him is unbearably uncomfortable, there is not enough reason for him to resist, to protest. Sadly, it is only the strong, self-confident, powerful horses who dare to resist misuse by open rebellion. Most horses suffer their fate without protest.

I therefore told this lady that if, in future, she would bring her mare along correctly and with the necessary patience, then this problem would soon be a thing of the past.

To school a young horse to be a riding horse means to prepare him thoroughly through ground work and work in-hand, so that at the first mounting you have the impression that the horse has already been ridden-in. There should be no sign of protest or rebellion. On the contrary, all the sensitive aids with which you have worked before can now be carried over to riding. In fact, 90 per cent of correct, horse-oriented riding-in takes place on the ground.

The time bombs

The interesting thing about all of this is that the horses who are not ridden-in but rather broken-in, or 'tortured-in', react like small time bombs and, as a rule, do not explode for six months to a year later. 'Until now everything worked so well and suddenly . . . !' 'She was the sweetest horse. As a three-year-old she was already being ridden across country, went out hunting or to shows and now . . .' etc. This is precisely the problem! And now the point has come where the pain is so strong it outweighs the horse's good nature. Hollowing the back no longer does any good, getting strung out and grinding the teeth does not help any more, now only rebellion remains.

What Birgit and Doris are demonstrating here in such an unrestrained way is obviously fun for both of them. What can be learnt from this kind of play, and, above all, what can be felt, are the many different pushing and pulling forces which unevenly stress the body during circular movement. The same thing happens during lunge work when too strong a contact is taken on the lunge, when it is no longer transmitting subtle signals but is used instead to keep the horse on a track, to hold him back or to stop him. When this happens the exercise is not nearly as much fun for the horse as it is for these two ladies, lungeing becomes an exercise of dubious value, harmful to the health of the horse.

The horse at liberty in the picadero

Although we work a horse on the lunge in the picadero from time to time, and although he travels more or less in a circle for most of the exercises, the exercises described here have little in common with lunging as we know it. Many maintain that lungeing is harmful to the soundness of the horse and also does not further the progress in dressage training. I agree with this because the way lungeing is commonly done can only be harmful.

Try a small experiment. At a gentle trotting speed, run in a circle with a diameter of 4–5 m (13–16 ft). This demands some dexterity but can be accomplished quite easily if you manage to balance yourself. Now ask someone to hold your inside hand and resume trotting. This time it will be more difficult for you to find your own equilibrium and to maintain it. You will also establish that a constant push and pull tension is travelling through your entire body and is now making itself felt in some body parts much more than in others. This is what happens with ordinary lunge work.

One of the most important goals of our work in the picadero is the development of the horse's balance. But that is exactly what is visibly disrupted the moment the trainer finds it necessary to tighten his hold on the lunge line. The horse then mobilizes his counter push/pull forces, which not only disturb his overall balance but also throw him heavily on the forehand. In addition, there is hardly anything more boring for a horse than running around in a circle, as you can imagine.

Our work in the picadero, therefore, differs in many ways from ordinary lunge work. It effects a complete and fundamental gymnasticizing of the horse, develops his lateral bending and horizontal flexion. It furthers the dominance/trust relationship, builds endurance and strength, improves reaction time and the general readiness to work and, finally, teaches both human and horse to communicate with one another through the use of the finest, most subtle body language.

Most importantly however, the work in the picadero can be structured so that the horse, through the work at liberty, adapts to the stresses of movement in his own way, but nevertheless remains within our control, within our sphere of influence. An extra bonus is that the horse retains his sense of joy and fun throughout the work.

With dance goes music

Music has an extraordinarily enlivening, soothing, and in every way positive, influence on the horse, and obviously on us as well. Whenever possible, work with background music. The type of music you choose to play can be adapted to the character of the horse and the nature of the exercises.

Once again Gabi with her warmblood mare doing free work in the picadero. The mare is carrying herself correctly and is well-balanced with her equilibrium appropriate to the exercise. Gabi has taken a position behind the horse, a position appropriate to the lead stallion in a wild herd.

The basic triangle

Nearly all of the following exercises have as their foundation a more or less exact right-angled triangle formed by the horseman's positioning relative to the horse.

The circle which the horse describes, at least in the early stages of the work, is determined by the boundaries of the picadero. In the centre of the picadero, the horseman describes a smaller circle of 1–2 m (3 ft 3 in – 6 ft 6 in) in diameter.

The principle of the 'moving trainer' in lunge work is found in all of the natural, horse-oriented schools of training. It is also a very important element in our work. If I stand rigid and motionless at the centre, then I have no way of transmitting information to the horse with my own

rhythm and tempo. I am forced to depend on the push and pull of whip and lunge. The most important element of communication, the interplay of demonstration and imitation, the body language, is shut off right from the start.

The second important reason for active movement on the horseman's part is also simple and logical. By moving on a small circle, I can, at any time, alter my position relative to the horse. So, I can, in a very subtle way, respond to every conceivable need in all circumstances. Finally, I can assume any dominant and driving position that a lead stallion in a wild herd can take.

This basic triangle is the foundation for our lunge work. In this position you send

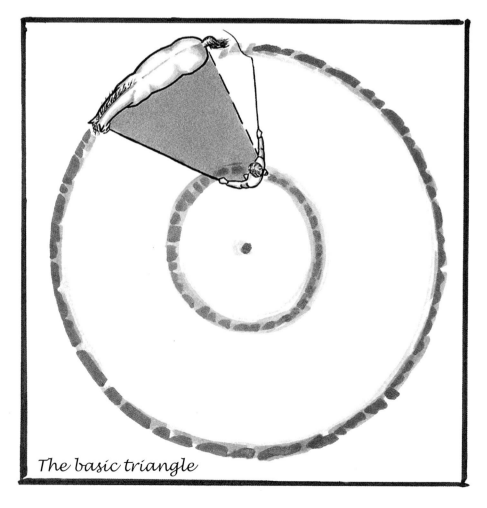

The basic triangle

These two photographs show the position of the horseman in the basic triangle. In the work in the picadero, and later out in the open, the maintenance of this position has great meaning. The shoulder of the horseman should always form a right angle with the croup of the horse.

elicit specific responses from the horse which can, in the more advanced work, be deliberately asked for. If you ask for them subconsciously though, by inadvertently changing your position, these responses will always disrupt the smooth flow of the work. Therefore, get a friend to watch you from time to time so that the consistency of your position can be checked. Correct positioning is essential and in the beginning it is not always so easy to maintain the triangle. The illustration on page 100 and the photographs on this page show very precisely the correct position relative to the horse. On a circle left you hold the lunge whip in your right hand, later you will be holding just a short whip. Your body and your eyes are on your horse's centre of gravity, looking toward the withers. The most important point is that **your right shoulder should always be at the level of the croup**, so that the whip is held several centimetres behind the tail, but without ever inadvertently touching the horse.

your horse ahead of you. He must perform all the required exercises on his own. This point is essential to the success of the work. Even minor changes in your position will

The first lesson in the picadero

Here we see Heide in the first practice session in the picadero. Again, everything is not as easy as it seems at first glance. Through the previous work our horses have already become pretty sensitized, so they react to every irregularity in our body movement. It is important that we move on our leading circle in a very regular tempo, that we always maintain the basic triangle, and that we stay at the horse's croup.

Lead your horse, as previously instructed, into the picadero. Now take off the halter and give him **several minutes of freedom**. You should do that before every training session to give the horse a chance to really stretch himself and, above all, to roll. That lightens the atmosphere and puts the workplace in a friendly light from the very beginning. If the horse is to be put in his stable after the session, then he should be given another chance to roll when the work is done.

A quick flick of the lunge whip and your horse will be trotting on a more or less correct circle. Now take your correct position with your shoulder at the level of the horse's croup, hold the whip at about the height of the croup and begin **striding** a small circle. When I say 'striding' I mean exactly that, not shuffling.

The beauty and regularity of your gait will carry over to your horse and, of course, the reverse is true as well.

This work in the picadero has nothing to do with 'letting the horse move around a bit'. It is highly concentrated and meaningful work. Therefore, sessions are only five to fifteen minutes long.

Our work is not routine

We can only expect the degree of sensitivity from our horse that we show him. We can only expect the degree of concentration from him that we ourselves demonstrate. The work with horses begins here, **with ourselves**.

I always capture what happens in my courses with a video camera, a practice that I would like to persuade you to follow. It is hard to believe the things that the video shows up. The reactions and the carriage of the horses are nearly always mirror images of the actions and the bearing of the horsemen. A horse always tells the truth, frequently mercilessly.

Far left
In my courses it has proven valuable to first try all the exercises without a horse. It is also good experience for the person playing the part of the horse, because they can really recognize which signals truly help and which are more of a hindrance because they create confusion. Here we see Anja and Gisela in the picadero. The person playing 'horse' is about one horse's length ahead in order to simulate the basic triangle. In order to make a precise circle more easily, it is very helpful, in the beginning, to mark the mid-point. Here we have used a red lead rope for that purpose.

Left
In the first photo we see Barbara in the correct position in relation to the horse. She is very focussed and her vigorous walk carries over to the horse. A short crouching jump toward the horse signals him to step under more sharply with the hindquarters and to remain standing in a nice square halt. Here the strength of the gesture is less significant than its correctness and the emphatic delivery. If the horse halts, we should wait several seconds before walking on again. It is important that during this waiting time we too remain standing absolutely still.

Barbara with her Friesian gelding in an improvised picadero. In my experience, Friesians are among the most intelligent horses of all and his gelding quickly became enthusiastic about the work.

In this sequence Barbara maintains her position in the basic triangle very well. Up to this point, the Friesian had had very little correct work. Because of this he is not correctly bent on the circle and even travels turned to the outside. It would be totally wrong to give in to the urge to change this temporary condition with the help of some sort of mechanical aids. Doing that would disturb the horse's free natural development and would surely throw him into the forehand (*see* Cause, effect, illusion). Through the consistent work in- hand and in the picadero this incorrect posture will disappear automatically and without additional effort on our part.

The horse halted promptly after a small gesture from Barbara, and the last four photographs show her standing motionless during the 'halt' phase. It is always amazing to see how nervous and even disobedient horses respond to these signals and even halt on cue.

The gait for these first exercises is the trot. Now ask for the first halt; out of the regular flowing movement take an emphatic step forward and move into a slight crouch. Your horse halts, and should stand, collected on the hindquarters. Remain standing motionless for five to ten seconds, then slowly resume walking in a comfortable posture and, again, give the horse a short signal to resume trotting. After a few times around at a quiet trot, repeat this exercise once, maybe twice, more and then work the horse the same way in the other direction. Did that not work well? Was it not simple?

'Help, my horse won't stand still!', or, all the things that can go wrong

Let us look at all the snags we may encounter.

1. The horse will not trot rhythmically, does not trot purely, or repeatedly breaks gait into walk or canter.

An unschooled or barely schooled horse tends to do these things; he has not yet developed his concentration and so runs ahead of himself. Nevertheless, you have at hand the methods to effect change.

If your horse does respond as above, then consider two points carefully.

First, you are probably not remaining truly and constantly at croup level. Your position most likely swings somewhere between the croup and withers. Your horse notices this immediately and responds with irregularities or unevenness in his gait.

Second, you probably lack the appropriate tempo and, perhaps, also lack 'pushing power'. Pushing power means a clear energetic movement that will keep the horse in an active, lively forward gait. The steps that you take on your inner circle are, of necessity, rather small. They must, therefore, be accentuated and very powerful. Bring all of your own power and personal presence to your work with your horse and work to increase these qualities in every session.

At this point in the schooling, to bring your horse out of the canter and into the trot, first bring him to a complete halt as you have already practised and then ask him to trot on again. You can, of course, try to get the desired transition directly with a half-halt.

We all have a lot of fun at the seminars, but that should not be allowed to interfere with our concentration on our work. Heide (below left) is unfocussed and not fully 'present' – traits mirrored by her horse. In such situations, the work is not only useless, but it is also likely to set things back.

In the second photograph (below right) Heide has regained her concentration, her position is correct, and the horse is attentive and also going correctly.

In the sequence on the right we see Kerstin with her mare, who is as nervous as she is nice. Kerstin had no problem halting the horse, but after only a split second's pause, the mare would turn and canter off in the other direction. Kerstin did the only correct thing and again gave her an emphatic halt signal by stepping toward her in a crouch. The whole episode was repeated several more times and, finally, because of Kerstin's consistency, even this mare stood motionless on the spot.

The effects on the subsequent behaviour of the mare were enormous. The dominance relationship changed instantly in Kerstin's favour, and the mare was visibly quieter. The trump card that horsemen hold by doing this kind of work is that we can dominate the horse and keep him within his set boundaries without any artificial, mechanical aids. That makes an enormous impression on the horse.

2. My horse simply will not halt!

Stubborn and thick-skinned horses – or those who have already been totally dulled – do not respond easily to subtle sensitive aids. The only solution is, no, not the slaughterhouse, but to continue the work with total consistency, do not despair and be patient. In the end it always works! But it is the ultimate test of your own character. Just when you have worked yourself into a lather, hopping around the animal like Rumpelstilskin and are wracking your brains for the butcher's telephone number, then, at that moment, your equine steamroller suddenly halts and asks with his naïve, goofy expression: 'Didn't I do that nicely?' Finally, when you are near to tears, only one thing remains for you to do: praise, praise, praise! Life can be so very hard!

3. My horse overreacts. He will not halt, but storms off in a frenzy in response to my halt signal.

These sensitive horses are actually my favourites. Usually, just making the halt signal more subtle is enough to stop the overreaction but please make certain your signal is still emphatic, 'impulsive', otherwise the horse will just wind down rather than coming to a decisive halt on the haunches.

4. My horse halts, but does not stand quietly.

For a horse unaccustomed to standing, this is not so easy. If the horse begins to walk without having been given a command to do so, most of the time it is because the horseman himself is not standing still. When the horse walks off of his own volition, give another clear halt command and, holding the whip in front of him, keep him within his boundaries.

5. Changing directions

To perform clean correct changes of rein through the circle, let alone with only subtle body signals, is something that requires correct technique, practice and confidence. We will get to the technique later on. To start, it is enough if, with the help of the whip, you manage to move your horse around to continue work in the other direction. Stay gentle, and touch your horse, either with your hand or the whip. At the beginning the horse will probably turn on his haunches and, at this point, that is fine.

Some more rules and suggestions

- During the work in the picadero, in fact during all your work, do not allow yourself to be disturbed. Allow spectators only on rare occasions. Most of the time they are a disturbance and distract you and your horse.
- Keep your work sessions short – five to twenty minutes – and always stop immediately when an exercise has gone particularly well.
- Work with your horse only when you are feeling rested, 'friendly' and in a good mood. Every time you feel anger rising do your best to control it and end the session before it is too late.
- If at some point you find yourself at your wit's end, it does not matter. Even when you become a great master you will encounter this situation over and over again. What do you do? At first, do nothing. Wait until you can get help, or until your intuition tells you how to proceed. That will usually be the right way to go. The main thing is that you do not force anything. You have all the time in the world, and no one is stopping you from taking two steps back. Rid yourself of ambition; it poisons any work you do with horses.

Are gymnastics only for the horse?

is important that we find a beautiful spot for our exercises so that we not only nurture our body, but also our eyes and our soul. To begin, we stretch and shake ourselves to our heart's content. Especially important is the loosening of each of the limbs individually. Britta lets us observe her morning exercises. In the first picture we see the basic position: the feet are parallel and about shoulder-width apart. In this first phase we will loosen-up, breathe, get the circulation going and warm up.

The next two photos show an exercise which is very important and which is also very relaxing and soothing. Without changing the position of the feet, swing round from one side to the other as shown. It is important that, while doing this, you breathe quietly and find your own pendulum rhythm. Success is not measured by cracking and popping joints; the entire spine, the pelvis, the whole body down to the heels, should be gently moved, loosened, and stretched.

Everything we do should be pleasant, never painful, and should never push or tax us beyond our capacity, even minimally. The limits of our ability will slowly, gradually expand through this work. Never overstep your limits because that will turn something sensible and beneficial into useless drudgery and may even be harmful to your health. As with everything else, proceed with care and patience.

We have already said a great deal about gymnastics for the horse. Now it is time to talk about rider fitness.

Riding is movement and harmony. Incorrect riding is strain and torment.

Should we ask our horses to carry us if we ourselves are not limber, fit and dexterous? No, we should not.

We need to be able to feel the movement of the horse correctly (more on that in a later chapter). Certain muscles must be well and powerfully developed in order to make truly harmonious riding possible. We need to be in good condition, have the ability to move our body parts independently and have muscles fit for use.

With gymnastics, as with so many other things; if it is badly done it is more harmful than helpful. I tend to follow the old-fashioned methods rather than modern trends, which change all too quickly and, as a rule, do not have a long history of success: hours of running through the woods, hours of lifting weights, doing aerobics, etc. In my experience with body movement in the theatre and the horse world, less is more!

For both horses and humans, a good work out is much less a question of time than of intensity!. Several minutes a day are actually enough to keep me sensibly fit.

Muscle building has nothing to do with endless repetition, with slaving away for hours at a time and overburdening yourself, but rather with reaching your maximum performance potential quickly. For the horse, for example, three correct canter departs from a rein-back followed by two or three strides of canter are enough, and will bring better condition and more muscle development than hours of lungeing and other work.

The isometric exercises shown on pages

Top row Please do this exercise very, very slowly and, most importantly, be sure to keep your knees slightly bent; do *not* under any circumstances lock your knees! Neither is it necessary that you bend over or hang down as far as possible. What is important is that you are relaxed and comfortable in the basic bending-over position with your head and shoulders slightly swinging, and that you hold this position for a moment while you quietly take a breath in and then exhale. Now, concentrate on your pelvis and, from there, slowly, joint by joint, bring yourself into an upright position. Head and shoulders remain passive and completely loose until the end. When you are totally upright, take a deep, quiet breath in, exhale, then slowly bring your arms forward, up, and let them lead your whole upper body into a backward bend. You can repeat this exercise two or three times depending on your mood and inclination. Follow your intuition. These exercises are suggestions which can be easily expanded upon and varied, and which you can use at your discretion. The basic selection is intended to increase stamina, develop muscles and supple the body, all in a balanced way.

Bottom row By now you should be fairly limber. The spine has been flexed horizontally and vertically and lightly swung. Now you want to concentrate on the legs and pelvis. Again, place your feet parallel to each other but this time somewhat further than shoulder width apart. From this position, bend first one knee, then the other, as shown. Bend the knee only as far, and only for as long, as it remains comfortable.

After a short pause we go from this position to the ground, supported by our hands as shown in the photo. We remain in this position for a moment, taking a quiet, deep breath in and out. During these moments it is good to turn our awareness to the sights, scents and sounds of our surroundings. That way, your in-breath will expand your lungs more and your exhalation, actually more important that the inhalation, will be more complete. Turning your awareness to your surroundings and breathing is a small but highly effective trick for many situations in life. In times of unrest, stress, anger or fatigue, the first thing to suffer is quiet breathing. If, in such situations, you 'turn-off' for a few seconds and focus your sense of smell on a nearby plant, or the fragrant spring or autumn air, afterwards you will see things quite differently.

Now, imagine that your hips are being held by a thick, heavy rope and are slowly being pulled upward. In this position, pause a moment and quietly, consciously breathe.

would now like to describe some exercises which work our musculature in a very gentle way. Muscles do not exist only to lift heavy things or to hit someone! They have many other jobs within the whole body structure; they support and assist the entire bone, tendon, ligament and joint apparatus. Developed muscles are therefore important for everyone but particularly important for those of us who want to take on the muscular burden of riding.

The isometric exercises shown here take, altogether, no more than five minutes but, if done once or twice daily, they will strengthen the entire muscle system in a sensible way.

Top row   In the first photo we see Britta in a seemingly 'pitiful' pose. However, that pose is not only, to a greater or lesser degree, the carriage we need to adopt to move as one with a horse, it is also the position that is the foundation stance of many of the eastern martial arts. While the position can be more or less perfect, it is important for riders that the knees are slightly bent and elastic, and that the hips are pushed slightly forward, thus lightly rounding the spine, and that the feet are shoulder-width apart and parallel to each other.

This basic position is the starting position for the following exercises. As shown in the second photo, press the palms of your

hands together (note the position of the elbows) with slow, steady pressure until, after about five seconds, you have reached your maximum capacity, then, just hold for five seconds at this level. By doing that you have worked a large portion of your upper arm, shoulder, and chest muscles enough for one day.

Breathe quietly and regularly.

Be sure your body stays loose and without any tension, use only the muscle groups needed for the specific exercises.

Now let your arms relax and loosen yourself up a bit. After a short pause, go to the next exercise. Each exercise is done only once!

In the third photo we see how Britta has clasped her

fingers in order to 'pull them apart'. Again the pressure (pull) is steadily increased for five seconds until the maximum is reached and then held for five seconds.

Bottom row   In the fourth photo, Britta's hands are placed behind her back at hip level, her fingers are clasped and, as above, she gradually increases the pressure, then holds at the maximum.

Next her palm is on the side of her hip (do both sides) and, finally, she works with one fist on top of another. The same pressure is applied for these last two exercises as for the others.

After these static exercises it makes sense to come back into a pleasant relaxed state through some slow, careful circling of the hips and shoulders (photos 1 and 2).

Now you can do two important energy exercises. You have seen how an angry gorilla beats himself on the chest with his two fists; not only is this a demonstration of power but there is also, in fact, a good reason for this display. Under the breast bone, where the ribs come together, is an important group of nerves, the solar plexus. Very lightly beat your breastbone for up to two minutes. Incorporated into an exercise programme like this one, or just done in a spare moment, this has an unbelievably energizing effect. Try it! For the ancient Greeks, the Chinese and the Indians the main energy of the body is in the centre, about one hand's width below your navel. This energy is nurtured through the organ complex of the kidney and the bladder, consequently, a kidney massage, the same or similar to those practised by many ancient cultures is beneficial, rub, or lightly beat, your back with both hands in the area of your kidneys (photo 4).

I find the exercise illustrated in the fifth photo particularly important. In the position shown, roll your pelvis to the left and then to the right several times. Breathe consciously and deeply, and do the exercise slowly and quietly.

The remaining three exercises are very clearly illustrated by the photos.

107–111 have been developed by modern research, supported by old traditions, but let us briefly discuss the muscle groups that are particularly important for riders. The seat (more on this later) we assume is a relaxed, comfortable, **natural seat**. With this natural seat we can absorb all the movements of the horse and it allows a permanent swing of the lower spine. This mobile part of the spine is supported by the lumbar muscles. If these muscles are not well developed, the lower spine cannot move freely because it must carry the body's entire burden. Many people today have back problems and pain in this area because insufficient physical activity has led to the deterioration of this natural supportive girdle resulting in overtaxing of the lower back.

A good seat on a horse is dependent on the condition and development of these muscles and a good seat on a horse also serves to strengthen this whole muscle group. The trick is to develop what I call 'tense relaxation', which allows the rider to sit relaxed, yet have the necessary stability.

The photos on pages 107–111 show you a small, but very important, selection of exercises specifically intended for riding that I have been teaching in my clinics for years.

Someone who practises Tai chi, bellydancing, yoga, or Feldenkrais movement in addition to riding, will find that their riding benefits from these activities, providing they have a good teacher and they do not overdo it. Let us approach our work sensibly and forever put aside ambition.

Half-halt from the ground

At this point, it is probably very easy for you to work your horse in the picadero at all gaits. Each upward transition to the next gait is connected to the appropriate voice command and a movement of the whip. You begin to rely less and less on the voice, so that, after a short time, your horse responds solely to the movement of the whip.

The lunge whip and later the driving whip (or dressage whip or in-hand whip) are held, at the beginning, at the height of the fetlock in walk, at the height of the knee in trot, and at the height of the dock in canter. Continually refine even these aids so that, finally, a barely perceptible lift of the whip is enough to elicit the desired reaction from the horse.

We do this not to make our work easier or our lives more comfortable. Through these foundation-building exercises the horse learns to quickly and consistently respond to the finest signals but this is not an end in itself. More importantly, the horse carries over this positive habit to everything else, including all future work under saddle. Everything is geared to make the horse more and more sensitive and to prepare him for collection on a loose rein, for being ridden with minute body signals.

The half-halt develops from the full halt, that is, you simply signal with a crouch and at the same time you shorten your own stride with a very distinct, slower step. For example, your horse is in regular, rhythmic trot, from your own relatively quick stride, take one more powerful step thereby going slightly into the crouch, and then walk on, more obviously slowly. Naturally, it takes feel to get exactly the right effect. At the same time, lower the whip. The whip now becomes a secondary aid because a collected shortening of your

horse's stride is eventually accomplished through a body signal which, though it becomes more and more refined, cannot be dispensed with.

The phenomenon of the half-halt will become clearer and more succinct in the next section (The Position Circle as an element of balance). The position that the horseman takes decides not only his degree of dominance (this has been covered in the previous chapters), but it is also a fine and subtle means of regulating and directing the movement of the horse.

Important. Please note.

If your horse, in response to a requested half-halt, goes from trot to halt, rather than into the walk, *do not* ask him to walk on again right away by raising the whip. On the contrary, you must praise your horse because he interpreted your subtle cue as a command to halt.

If you do not praise your horse at this point, then he may well ignore the next body signal to halt. So, should your horse react to your half-halt command by coming to a complete halt, you stand still too and act as though a halt was exactly what you had in mind. When you next ask for a half-halt, reduce and refine your body signal still further, and continue to do that until your horse realizes what you want.

This point is quite difficult in practice. It is important that the horse is not confused, so I hope that I have made the reasons for praising him in these circumstances very clear.

The Position Circle as an element of balance

When we move from the groundwork to riding we will talk about how the rider can establish and support the all-important balance by the backward and forward movement of his upper body, which is also the most important signal for the full and half-halt. In the same way, the Position Circle gives me the possibility of establishing the required balance whether 'driving' or 'braking' in the work on the ground. It is an indispensable aid to communication.

Even up to High School level, these positions are used for driving and braking and, as signals, are refined continually.

Position 1 We have already discussed this position. In the work on the circle, the horseman is most often on the line that goes through this point.

Position 2 Moving into this position has the effect of increasing drive and collection. The horseman takes this position when these are required, and also when a new signal is to follow, perhaps for a halt or for a change of direction. This request for increased driving and collection should precede each new command, in order to get the horse's attention and prepare him.

Without changing the accentuation of my steps, I shorten them very slightly in order to position myself somewhat further behind the horse. Then I hold this position for a moment in order to give the next signal. These are flowing movements which an observer can barely perceive. Attention to such small details as the work progresses improves the picture more and more, and adds up to a perfect whole.

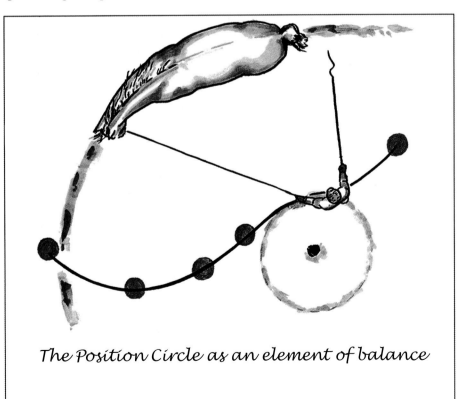

The Position Circle as an element of balance

Position 3 If the horseman finds himself in this area, his position has the effect of braking, but without collection. However, the deliberate moving from Position 1 to Position 3 has a collecting effect because that is the exact direction of movement for the full and half-halt. For example, in order to bring a horse from trot to walk we give the signal for a half-halt. If we are successful, it is possible that a young, energetic horse will want to go back into trot or canter right away. In order to prevent this, the horseman moves into the area of Position 3 and stays there until the horse maintains the requested action. Once he has, the horseman moves back to Position 1.

As a rule, Position 3 is also the position a horseman is in after a successful halt. To keep a young, uneducated, inattentive horse standing still, it may be necessary to move in the direction of Position 4, 5 or even 6.

Standing still in one spot on the circle for up to ten minutes or even longer, is an exercise I often ask of impatient or highly-strung horses. This has a tremendously focussing, collecting, calming and trust-building effect. I do not do this by fighting the horse or by using mechanical aids but exclusively by the subtle method of body positioning.

Positions 4, 5 and 6 As implied, the influence of these positions is one of braking which increases as we move closer to Position 6.

As a rule, we must, whenever possible, position ourselves in the area of Position 1. All the other positions are for temporary clarification of an exercise or for very specific, momentary tasks.

Position 5, or even 6, is the one the horseman will take up when he begins to teach the horse to back up on a circle. If we proceed logically and consistently, then, in a short time, the horse will willingly back up, without problems, even if we are in Position 1.

Positions 4 to 6 are those which the horseman assumes in the continuing exercises of lateral movements and piaffe.

In the course of time you will develop a very fine feel for which position will best support your horse at any particular moment. Always be aware that this should not be hurried. Your intuition will put you on the right path: slowly, better and better, and in perfect peace.

Some more vital factors

- The canter is a gait that is comparatively taxing for the horse, especially on a fairly large circle. If, during the early exercises, your horse decides to canter, just accept it and wait until he comes down to a trot or walk of his own accord. **You should ask for the canter only after he has been working correctly at the walk, and especially trot, for a number of weeks.** It is the preparatory work that will gymnasticize and collect the horse and bring him into balance so that he can be worked progressively in canter. To clarify this point: it is no problem to get a horse to canter, however, it is important to wait for the time when it is **useful** to the horse to do this. If the horse is ready for canter work on the circle, then he will take the gait with only the slightest, most subtle encouragement. He will jump into the depart powerfully and joyfully and will stay in collected canter effortlessly. If there is the least bit of difficulty with the canter, it is always a sign that he has been asked too soon.
- Do not forget to prepare the horse for each new signal with a small verbal cue. A short 'attention' or 'ready' will get your horse's attention and your signal will not startle him.
- Please do not forget to praise!

- I know I am repeating myself, but I do so deliberately: **please do not ask too much of your horse**. A horse should never be sweating when he finishes work. That is an unacceptable overtaxing. A horse is capable of the greatest effort but he should be trained and conditioned in advance. Make the work as varied as possible. Give your horse interesting, systematic, sensible work that is meaningful to his development, not hours and hours of drudgery.

- The halts from trot and canter will get better and better, soon they will look really spectacular. But be careful! Practise halts out of walk and trot, **not canter**! The purpose is to gymnasticize the horse, not wear him out or break him down. Please do not make a spectacle of the halt the way many Western riders do, because it is done at the expense of your horse. There is no standard rule for these things. Your good sense, your love of horses and your intuition must determine the standard at each moment. For a true horseman this is self-evident. We must examine ourselves and our motives, again and again.

In order not to lose sight of the whole, we take a careful look into the future

Collected riding on a loose rein means to work a horse in such a way that he finds and maintains his equilibrium on his own. It is analogous to this: for twenty years you have been trying to pound a nail into the wall holding the hammer in your left hand. Then someone comes along and says, 'Why not hold the hammer in your right hand?' You see the light and from then on you always hold the hammer in your right hand. That is what we are trying to do in our work with horses. Laugh if you will but it works! We show the horses how they should hold the hammer in the future. We show them that it is much more comfortable and less stressful to their bodies to carry their weight on the hindquarters. Once the horses understand this, it is no longer necessary to continually remind them. They will do it automatically. With our help, the horse searches for the point at which movement is most comfortable, and that is when the weight is taken over to the hindquarters, i.e. collection. We have already begun this process: we have established the dominance/trust relationship, we can halt our horse on the hindquarters and we can, through the half-halt, shorten his stride in collection.

Now we must help our horse to achieve even more flexion so that the inner hind leg steps more strongly under the centre of gravity. Greater flexion on small circles is, however, something we do not want to force because, if we tighten the lunge line or the reins, all we achieve is the falling out of the croup and the horse falls on the forehand. Soon our horse will be able to execute even small circles very nicely.

This all leads to an exercise which, when **correctly done**, presents a key lesson under saddle as well as in the work in-hand. This exercise is **shoulder-in**. If we have prepared our horse well, this movement should be a fairly simple next step. This exercise is valuable and beautiful in the hands of those who understand it.

Parallel to the development of the shoulder-in in-hand we also try to improve and perfect the **change through the circle**, in the picadero and on the lunge line. Eventually, we can widen the boundaries of the picadero and, soon thereafter, work our horse on the lunge in the open.

At this point the horse has learned to accept the loosely hanging lunge line as a fine connection to us and to react to subtle body language, rather than pushing and pulling. At this point we will also develop full and half-halts on horseback without rein aids and we will show our horse, through simple exercises, how to turn by mere weight and leg aids.

At the end of this phase we will be able to turn and stop our horse without any rein aids whatsoever, using these only for occasional support and as signals to perfect the work.

In none of these schooling phases are the reins used with any lasting contact. We learn to maintain a supple, natural seat on the horse thus finding our way into his movement so that our upper body becomes a quiet balance-giving mechanism for transmitting the subtlest aids.

If the horse moves with us through all turns and voltes because of our body language and leg aids alone, then it is easy to begin the practice of shoulder-in under the rider. The horse is clearly prepared and ready for it, and a slight shift in weight and a light leg aid will be enough for him to offer us the first crossing steps of the hind legs in shoulder-in.

Through plenty of schooling in-hand and the many preparatory exercises without reins, our horse has become so sensitive that even in the development of the lateral movements the reins serve only to give an occasional signal.

Our horse is also working perfectly from the fourth leading position (when the horseman is at the level of the croup) and quiet signals are enough to get the horse to back up expressively, to trot powerfully on, and to be brought to a collected halt. Through this work the horse becomes ever more compact, until out of the collected backing-up and upon receiving a small driving and braking gesture, he offers the first steps of piaffe.

This book ends with the shoulder-in exercise because, at that point, you will have done all the foundation work to collect a horse on a loose rein and, thus, ride in collection.

All the exercises that build upon this foundation further refine the work and continue to strengthen and supple the horse, but they are not prerequisites for gymnasticizing a horse and keeping him sound for riding. So, continue perfecting the exercises leading up to this point, for the good of your horse.

The horse on a thread: the work on the lunge

Have you noticed that we have approached this work completely the opposite way from the usual way? First we worked the horse at liberty and, now that everything is working so beautifully, we start to use the lunge.

I do not just use this approach in my courses, I always work horses this way. This method ensures that we humans learn to work first with the tools we have available – our bodies – and the horses learn to move freely and lightly, particularly when working with humans.

If we, as a next step to our work in the picadero, put our horse on the lunge, then it is only to develop another way of communicating subtle signals, the lunge is never used to pull or to reinforce a halt command. Nothing really changes for us in this work, it is for the horse to accustom himself to this fine connection with us. The lunge line hangs permanently in a slight loop. In the beginning phases, as shown here, the loop is quite large. In the third photo we see that all halts must continue to come through without the action of the lunge line.

From the start, the feeling of freedom is retained and remains an integral part of the horse's education, particularly out in the open.

There is a very important principle underlying the work with lead rope, reins, and lunge line: **we always work as though they were not available!**

When problems arise it must be possible to solve them without the lunge line and that is why the lunge comes into play so late in the game.

Do we even need it? Yes, we do. Not to halt the horse, not as a braking mechanism, not to pull, but as a means of giving very subtle signals that connect us to our horse.

The lunge line never drags on the ground and it is also never taut: it always loops softly which means that I can send my horse away from me and bring him closer, I can enlarge and reduce the circle as I wish, **without ever restricting his freedom of movement, without ever sending him onto his forehand by pushing and pulling**. Once he has learned this, you can take him outside on the lunge, working him in the open and sending him where you will; he will always keep this fine threadlike connection between the two of you and observe it scrupulously.

This is already quite an achievement in itself but it also has a great deal to do with collected riding on a loose rein because the horse will now respond in every situation, **without any sort of mechanical intervention**.

Now you can appreciate why the theme of dominance is so decisive for us because, by this point, at the latest, every form of resistance, even the most subliminal, must be absolutely forgotten. Now my horse must want to go where I wish. It must be a pleasure for him to be allowed to follow

Here we see Gabi lungeing her mare in the open. During the work in the picadero the horse learned to always respect and accept the fine connection to the human through a loosely looped lunge line. Only when this has been established with absolute certainty can we leave the picadero and continue our work outside. The photos show how evenly the mare is bent on the circle from head to tail and she is in total balance with even and regular gaits. Any tug or pull on the horse's head – however it is caused – would totally disrupt this harmony of movement. We horsemen only make suggestions – the horse is, and remains, unhindered and free in all his movements!

me. If at this point, the horse resists because he wants to eat or go to the mares or to his stall – in total opposition to what I had in mind – then a big piece of the work has been for nothing. Naturally the horse will, and is allowed to, continue to think of all those things, but I should have become more important to him!

The lunge line should be as light as possible, very fine and very pliant. Those that are commonly sold are wonderful but in my opinion, are particularly suited for High School work, by which time the horseman will have developed proficiency using the lunge. In a beginner's hands these flat lines regularly get tangled and you spend more time untangling them than with the horse. So a light rope makes everything much easier and we can concentrate fully on our horse and on what we are doing.

When we start the lunge work, we start by doing exactly what we have done on previous days: we make sure that our lunge line is looped softly and, most critically, that we are never tempted to pull! To learn that is our first and most important assignment.

Even if the horse changes direction, please do not pull. Once you are no longer becoming entangled in the lunge line and the whip lash during each change of direction, then the conditions are ripe for moving to the next step.

The work with the small stallion Fulano has, in the meantime, developed into 'playing with one another'. The horse has totally accepted the lunge line as a fine connection to me – he will never again take up on the lunge to the point of tautness. In the last photo it can be seen how the horse notices and responds to a slight lifting of the line.

The horse is often left to himself within the boundaries created by the lunge line. The dominance relationship has been so precisely established that the horse can even take positions 'forbidden' by the rules of the Position Circle.

Reducing and enlarging circles

Even on the now significantly smaller circle the fundamental rules and standards of the work in the picadero remain in effect. The position is still the basic triangle, and the lunge line is in a permanent soft loop. Through body language, light signals of the whip and the slight raising of the leading hand, the horse can now be turned and led unbelievably precisely. Two dancers in harmony, each thoughtfully attentive to the other, acting and reacting with soft transitions and then again with surprising reprises. Just as on the dance floor, the partners play with one another: they move apart only to find each other again in the next moment. Sometimes you use the entire space, working from the centre of the picadero, then you use the corners to develop the bend and prepare the horse for new, daring escapades. Now the horse challengingly lowers his expressive head, signaling an elegant change through that very small circle. The horseman responds to this suggestion by cocking his hips back – a powerful swing brings the large animal onto the other rein, then horse and horseman stand motionless for seconds, minutes as the silent tempo pulses rhythmically through both of them.

We begin in walk.

Our horse has accustomed himself to the loose line in the picadero and also in the earlier leading work. Now, when we move from Position 1 in the Position Circle to Position 2 – stepping slightly behind the horse and a bit closer to him – shortening the lunge line a bit but always leaving it slightly looped, then the horse will gradually make the circle smaller. To begin with we are satisfied with very little reduction of the circle and soon send the horse back to the outer circle by taking up our former position again, lengthening the lunge line and occasionally giving it a slight 'swing' so that the horse re-establishes his original positioning.

It is important to work the horse equally in both directions. After a few days it is easy to bring the horse to circle within 1–2 m (3 ft 3 in–6 ft 6 in) of us at a walk

and then to send him back to the outer circle without loss of rhythm or tempo.

If everything is going well, you can do this same exercise at trot. It will still be quite some time before you can reduce the circle at canter. The horse will let you know when he is ready for this by allowing himself to be brought easily on to a small circle if he is physically able to do so.

Important Always go back to working the horse at liberty in the picadero in between lunge sessions.

Before we turn to two exercises which are of great significance to our main theme – dancing with horses – namely, the shoulder-in and the change of rein through the circle, I would like to shed some light on something very important: how a horse learns.

How does a horse learn?

We know that a horse is a prey animal, a flight animal, but he only takes flight when the boss does! If there is danger in the vicinity, he will most probably be momentarily startled but, in a functioning herd, all the members will remain standing until the lead animal gives the signal for flight. These actions are reflexes, automatic reaction patterns, not considered behaviour. A human, or an animal, has learned something, **truly** learned something when a new pattern of behaviour has become second nature, when what has been learned follows the path of an automatic reaction.

A student driver needs to devote all his attention to performing all the required functions in the proper order. An experienced driver, however, will effortlessly manoeuver his vehicle through the heaviest traffic while turning his attention to a heated discussion; driving a car has become automatic, it follows a specific reaction pattern. That is what we would like to achieve with our horses.

For example, cocking the hip (which we will discuss in more detail later on) will elicit a natural halt response from the horse. He will execute it more or less promptly, that is, when this relatively weak stimulus is not being overpowered by another, stronger one. In a quiet arena, the signal will work but, outside, amid the hustle and bustle of life it most likely will not, particularly at the beginning. We want to be able to bring our horse to a halt with this signal under all circumstances, whenever necessary, even out of a full gallop. With the reins and an appropriately severe bit, we will almost always manage it but, our horse does not need to learn anything for that. If, however, we want to employ this very fine stimulus of cocking the hip then something very important needs to happen: the connection between this subtle signal of the rider and the unconditional halt must be so well established in an intrinsic reaction pattern that the correct response occurs automatically and subconsciously. If that is the case, then our horse has truly learned and this phase of training is truly established.

The illustration below clarifies this principle. First, something (the stimulus) occurs that registers in the brain, is processed there, and is then passed on to the motor functions so that the appropriate reaction can occur.

In the course of this learning process new neural pathways are created which, in the end, make the long passage through the brain and back unnecessary. The cock-

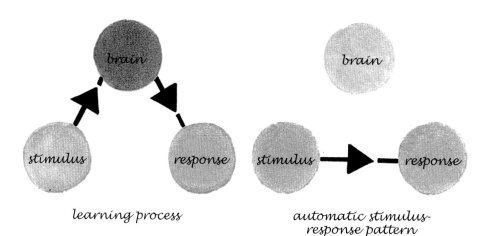

<table>
<tr><td>learning process</td><td>automatic stimulus-
response pattern</td></tr>
</table>

ing of the hips is the stimulus, the prompt halt is the response, which will now follow automatically. **Now the horse can no longer respond otherwise**, just like the experienced driver will automatically do the right thing in a dangerous situation and only afterwards think about what happened and how he responded.

A plaster cast for the nerves

Learning is a growth process, neural pathways must connect naturally at their own pace. When someone breaks an arm, it is encased in a plaster cast for several weeks. The arm needs to be kept still and protected from shocks and concussion. If you remove the cast a bit too soon, then the time already spent healing has most probably been wasted because, with the slightest strain, the arm will break again and, even worse, it will mend less well than the first time.

It is just like that with the learning process. If the nerve pathways are only partially complete and we rely on the result too soon then everything will fall apart and putting it together again will require considerably more effort than the first time around.

How do we proceed?

1. In peace, with concentration and in small stages. If we are simply spending time with our horses, playing around and having fun with each other, that is one thing but, if we are going to learn and have instruction, then we see to it that we have a quiet, peaceful, concentrated atmosphere.

2. We always go from the known to the unknown. This demands creativity and imagination from us, because we must follow a specific concept, a clear path. For example: on the lunge line the horse has learned to halt on cue. Now he needs to do this under saddle. What has already been learned, the known, will help us with this. We have an assistant stand in the middle of the arena who cocks his hip in the halt signal at exactly the same time that we, in the saddle, use the pelvis to give the halt cue.

These photos illustrate one of the elementary principles of horse training: the principle of always moving from the known to the unknown. Even the most nervous, anxious horse, will, within minutes, walk over a sheet of plastic for example, which nothing and no one would have got him near before. It is important, though, that an obvious 'bridge' is built which the horse can cross trustingly. If the horse has been led through a small pole alley and been given a reward at the end, then this area has become trusted and familiar. Now all that has to be done is to gradually bring the unfamiliar, the fearful, into his trusted and familiar routine, thus easing the horse's fear.

After a few minutes, the horse walks over a plastic sheet as though it were the most natural thing in the world.

The known supports the unknown, the horse connects the separate stimuli and responses with one another and **learns**.

Another simple but unbelievably effective example is the pole alley. Here, again, we go from the known to the unknown and use the principle of the stimulus-response pattern.

We use jump poles to lay out a lane about 60 cm (2 ft) wide and lead our horse through it a number of times, each time giving him a reward when he reaches the end. After four or five times a stimulus-response pattern has been created, namely: walk through the poles without a problem and receive a reward at the end.

Now I can put whatever I want in the lane: plastic bags, aluminium foil, etc. After only a few moments my horse learns to negotiate these things without any worries at all. The response pattern has become stronger, the positive experience counts for more than the fear of the obstacles.

Same sequence, same place

We should make everything as easy as possible for ourselves and, above all, for the horse! Whenever we can, we put little 'plaster casts' around the new neural pathways so that everything connects truly and solidly. Once it has come together it will last forever.

When we begin new exercises we do so at a specific time and place within the entire lesson structure. If a horse is to have his first lessons in shoulder-in, I will put this new exercise between the work on the circle and backing-up, for example. I will stick to this same sequence for several days so that, just through the rhythm of the work, the horse already has a learning aid, a 'plaster cast'. In addition, I have a very specific place for each exercise. If I go to point X or point Y with my horse then he knows that it is now time for Spanish Walk and now for shoulder-in. These small aids make the work so much easier for both human and horse. While doing this, I cannot violate the rule about making the work as interesting and varied as possible but our work is multi-faceted and, within this complex whole, fixed points for new exercises can be easily found.

Do not take off the cast too soon!

This is a very important point, and one that addresses an aspect of human nature. Naturally, the human is pleased when his horse has learned something. This often leads to the desire to show off this new trick or try it somewhere else. But then it

A very important learning goal is to make the desired responses a reflex as quickly as possible, so, I always take my horses to specific places for certain exercises, at least in the early phases. I had always worked on Spanish Walk with this stallion at a certain olive tree. As soon as we got near the spot he began swinging his forelegs, already knowing what I wanted of him in this special place. Naturally, you should not wait too long before changing the routine, otherwise you could end up with a riding horse that endangers both himself and his handler by anticipating, and going into, the move just because he has caught a glimpse of a bottle of olive oil!

goes sour, you yank and pull and excuse the whole embarrassment with a nervous laugh and a reference to show nerves.

The embarrassment, however, is not the problem. The problem is the work you have to do afterwards, because it will be much more difficult than before. We took the cast off too soon! The arm has broken again. Always be very careful with demonstrations. And if you cannot resist them, then at least demonstrate only those things that have been confirmed for a long, long, time and which are truly established. Do not, under any circumstances, demonstrate work from your current training programme because it could backfire badly.

The confounded fourth day

Something else we must know in order to understand the horse is that, in nature there are no linear processes, underlying everything is a more or less fixed cycle. Summer, winter; day, night. We are part of nature; horses are part of nature. If we choose to do the same thing day after day encased in steel and neon lights, turning night into day and winter into summer then that is down to us but the horse is still much more strongly bound to nature, he still lives deeply in these primal rhythms.

Learning is a natural, cyclical growth process which the horse is fully subjected to. **Learning happens in waves.** Today something works with my horse, tomorrow he acts as though he has never heard of this before. Does this make him a dumb animal? I do not believe so, I believe it is the confounded fourth day. It could also be the third or the fifth day. At any rate, it is the day on which the horse is at the low point of the wave or learning curve. This low point, however, is a little higher than the previous one and that is the sign of a **true learning sequence**.

It is these low points that show whether a horse has actually learned something. If I want to be certain that something will always work, then it must succeed precisely at these low points.

So, do not immediately scold and punish but, instead, remember that this reaction is absolutely natural and can even serve as a sign of true progress.

The creative pause

The creative pause also has to do with the natural rhythm of things. It is something which we all sense in ourselves but which we only too seldom can pursue or even want to pursue. Again and again, and everywhere in nature, we bump into the fundamental principle of priorities and discontinuity. Only the human being tries with every means to violate even this natural law. Learning happens on two levels, the conscious and the subconscious. Once the conscious level has done its part and absorbed the elementary principles, then what has been learnt must continue to permeate other levels of being. This requires a period of rest – a creative pause.

Depending on the horse, I work one to two weeks on a particular exercise and then I do not do it at all for the same length of time. When I begin the exercise again, it always goes better than when I left off.

The subconscious has worked for us and thereby deepened and strengthened the basics. Through this the work programme becomes not only richer in variation but its success is longer lasting.

Fear

Fear is the most primal and elemental experience for every living being. Fear blocks all other life expressions and actions. If the worst comes to the worst I can break-in a horse by putting him in a state of fear but, in those circumstances I cannot sensibly and meaningfully educate, school or develop him. I think this is the last time I need to make this point in this book.

The shoulder-in in-hand

Shoulder in, the initial stages of which I will describe in this chapter, is a prerequisite for the many High School exercises, as well as for our everyday collected riding (although basically there is no difference between the two).

Shoulder-in is an exercise which every rider should master. In fact, this exercise, correctly done, is an unbelievably effective way of gymasticizing and collecting a horse. But, as with everything else, you should approach the work carefully because, incorrectly done, shoulder-in would be useless at best and possibly even harmful.

The description of shoulder-in

Although the horse is moving on the track, his head and shoulders are facing into the arena. Depending on the degree of the angle of bend he will be moving on three or four tracks.

In a correctly executed shoulder-in the horse should bend evenly from his head to his dock. Also of vital importance is that, once in this position, in order to move forward, the horse must move his inside hind leg in front of the outside one, thus crossing his legs. He must step further under his body with his inside hind leg, lower his croup and flex his hocks; he must be collected. This exercise is beautifully designed to show the horse how comfortable and easy it is to displace his own weight, and that of the rider, back onto the hindquarters and carry the burden with flexed and suppled haunches. Once the horse has learnt this he will carry out this process more and more ably and independently. This will happen over a period of time and depends on the gentle introduction of the task. In time the horse will be so gymnasticized that the haunches develop the necessary carrying power and elasticity.

This exercise is introduced fairly early in the training by working on the shoulder-in in-hand. This has many advantages. We can lead the horse into this exercise very gradually so that he can find his own way into this exercise without the added weight of a rider. By working in-hand, we have, most importantly, a simple, easy way of teaching the horse to do this exercise independently and in self-carriage.

Shoulder-in on four and three tracks

This point is critical!

The horse should go sideways at a very specific angle to the track and cross his legs behind to do this. Many riders, understandably, try to achieve this desired position by a relatively strong pull on the reins and they maintain the pull for the duration of the exercise. Doing this, however, will throw the horse on his forehand, thus negating the original purpose of the exercise. This leads to even more pulling and dragging which, in the end, can only result in damage to the horse.

The illustration on page 54 shows Francois Robichon de la Guérinière (the riding master of Louis XV of France) in shoulder-in on a perfectly positioned and collected horse **on a loose rein!** In fact, it is only when it is performed in this way that the exercise makes any sense. The horse is unrestrained and can, by increased use of his haunches, develop his balance without having to struggle against disruptive outside forces.

At the end of this book I will try to describe how you achieve this in the saddle. The horse must have achieved a certain level of sensitivity as well as a certain degree of strength and suppleness and the rider must have a certain measure of 'feel'.

The work in-hand allows the desired goal to be reached with comparative ease and prepares the horse for the work under

We would usually use a halter and lead line to help us with this exercise in order to be able to give certain subtle signals. Here, however, Birgit demonstrates perfectly that shoulder-in can be executed solely by the horseman's choice of the correct position and the appropriate body language. We can see how Sami goes through the corner in shoulder-in as Birgit maintains the correct position. This particular moment demands great concentration and 'feel' in both human and horse. In the fifth photo we can see the correct bend of the horse's body. Sami is moving on four tracks. This photo also shows the prelude for the movement to progress through the next corner; the bend of the horse's body is accordingly more pronounced. It is important to hope that the horse is not almost straight as with leg-yielding. The very positive effects of this exercise are achieved only when the horse is bent evenly through the length of his body.

saddle. Once he has learned to do this exercise independently without a rider he will be able to do it more easily under saddle.

Under saddle or in-hand, when we are doing shoulder-in we must take care to maintain the proper angle. With an even bend from head to tail, the horse will, in the end, be moving on four tracks. If the angle is sharper, then, as a rule, the horse avoids the bend and the exercise deteriorates into mere leg-yielding which has virtually no collecting or gymnasticizing effect. If the angle is less sharp, as it is in modern dressage, then the horse needs to bend himself less and does not need to cross the hind legs or step more strongly under his body.

In all the previous exercises, we have seen how important the position of the horseman is by observing the response of the horse. In this exercise, however, correct position is absolutely critical. First, the position tells the horse exactly what angle is required and, secondly, it prevents the hindquarters from leaving the track. This exercise is not particularly strenuous for the horse if he has had the appropriate preparation, nevertheless, he will be inclined to avoid the effort the exercise demands, either by making the angle sharper or flatter, or by running forward. Both can be prevented, either by the rude employment of lead rope or bridle, or by sensitive body language.

In the photo sequence on page 125 Birgit shows us a perfect shoulder-in from the ground with the horse at liberty. It is merely her position relative to the horse, maintaining the exact angle, which gives the horse the necessary signals. These photos are good for demonstration purposes, but for serious schooling it is more sensible to use a lead rope which hangs loosely most of the time.

We start this exercise in the same way as we will later introduce shoulder-in under saddle. First we lead our horse through

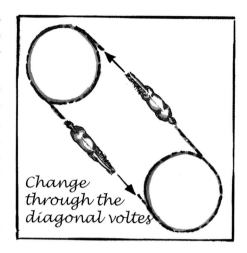

Change through the diagonal voltes

the picadero in the pattern pictured above. I call this pattern 'diagonal voltes' (in this case, to the left) because from a volte in one corner, I come diagonally across the arena, execute another volte in the opposite corner, and return again across the diagonal to my original corner. This exercise will also be ridden at a later stage.

In previous exercises, we have used a lifting of the leading hand to slow or even stop the horse. This signal has become so integrated into our natural communication that the horse will react sensitively to it in the following exercise.

Lead the horse through a volte in the corner three or four times then bring him straight across the diagonal to the opposite corner for another volte (*see* above). Once this has been done a few times the horse will begin to anticipate and adjust his body to go on to the next volte and this leads to the following. As soon as the horse is in an even bend and in position as pictured on page 127, we leave our basic triangle position by taking a quiet step forward so that we are at the level of the horse's withers. At the same time we slightly raise our leading hand in order to restrain the horse ensuring that the lead line continues to hang in a soft loop. Now we move energetically toward the horse as though we were going to ram his shoulder and the whip is brought forward from its original position behind the horse so that it can move lightly in the area of the flanks. The horse will now yield to us automatically and will move diagonally across the picadero in a perfect shoulder-in (*see* the photo sequence on page 184).

To begin with, the exercise may not be as perfect as we have described but, if we have worked carefully up to this point, our horse should at least give us pieces of the desired movement.

Problems that can arise

The horse pays no attention to the raised leading hand, he simply continues on his circle.

We can prevent this by stepping a bit further forward in our first attempts at this exercise, perhaps even in front of the horse. Please do not pull on the lead line, that would undermine the entire purpose of this exercise.

The angle of the shoulder-in is too sharp.

This happens quite frequently in the early stages because the horse tries, by all means, to avoid the effort of the correct bend. To prevent this, we must employ our body in a very conscious and focussed way. Our position in relation to the horse, the use of the leading hand and the whip, and the power of our forward movement, all of this must come together in a perfect, very harmonious way in order to get the horse to respond exactly as we wish. Even the first one or two steps of shoulder-in are a major

The shoulder-in in-hand

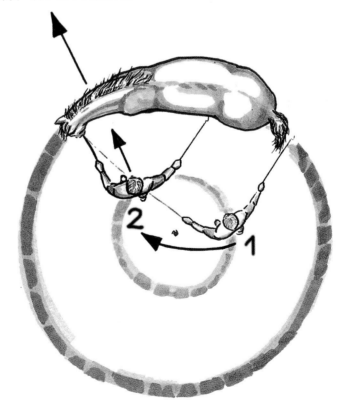

1. *starting position*
2. *position for introducing the shoulder-in*

success for us and for the horse. We stop the exercise immediately when we have them, we praise and reward the horse and we do not repeat this exercise again until the next day or the day after.

This exercise is so essential that it is perfectly in order to allow ourselves plenty of time to perfect it. It is important, though, that we apply ourselves to our practice with energy and strong intent, otherwise we will be left running in place getting nowhere. Because we do not punish, pull, drag or bellow, we are left only with communication via our bodies and, above all, our personal presence which is decisive in the game of power.

In the last chapter of this book I discuss in great detail how important variety is for the wellbeing of our horses and for the success of our work. When we are introducing and practising exercises like this one, this point is absolutely critical.

A horse that carries out this exercise correctly, especially at the very beginning, is working hard, even if it does not look like that. Impatience and insensitivity at this point can ruin much that has been previously achieved. To preserve the psychic equilibrium of our horse at its optimum level through what will be a long mutual journey of discovery, we change his routine. We play with him. We take him out into the countryside in-hand or under saddle. Then, when we turn again to further precise schooling, it is not a burdensome duty but rather another welcome change.

Play, advanced schooling, building up the dominance/trust relationship or simply idle time spent with one another, the boundaries dissolve and everything blends into a sensitive, harmonious togetherness.

Once the horse changes between the diagonal voltes in a beautiful shoulder-in, then we leave this fixed picadero pattern and fit the movement into our schooling-programme wherever we please.

When the horse is being led to his paddock, it is easy to ask him for a few steps of shoulder-in to either side and, before he turns his attention to his daily grazing, he has been wonderfully gymnasticized without even knowing it.

I cannot possibly end this chapter without going into an 'essential and weighty' argument about riding theory. I would like to discuss this particular 'problem' not as a separate entity but as an example of how rules, judging standards, and training philosophies suddenly evolve from what I believe is a fundamentally distorted point of view and are then viewed with the same awe and respect as mathematical axioms, immutable laws of nature, or holy relics. The problem I refer to is:

The rider's fear of the fourth track

Let us examine once again that being who in many riding disciplines, seems to have only a very subordinate place, namely, the horse. The 'exercise' of shoulder-in belongs, just like travers, piaffe, and passage to the natural behaviour of the horse in the wild, although the power of the movement and the brilliance of the execution grow, as a rule, in proportion to the horse's ranking in the herd.

A stallion guarding his charges from some distance will always be turning his head in one direction or the other in order to be observant, watchful and alert. But, he will not just be turning his head; more often than not this action occurs in a moderate to perfect shoulder-in position. Another example, which you will probably recognize from your own experience, is that a horse, particularly an agile, well-gymnasticized one, that courageously approaches a frightening object does not go straight at it. He usually stalks it at an angle, sideways, with his head turned toward the 'monster', in other words, toward the direction of movement thus executing a perfect half-pass. In this way he is perfectly positioned to turn on the haunches and take flight.

Who is going to tell these unschooled wild horses, who survive untouched by any culture and furthermore cannot even read, that these movements they are doing (shoulder-in) should, please, be done on three tracks otherwise they will fall on the forehand? That, at any rate, is what competition rules require and what is said in many current textbooks.

Let us look at this from a more detached perspective and agree that a loose horse can do what he pleases. He will always find his balance, because that is how nature has made him; the flight gallop is the only exception to this (*see* Flight or fight). The natural movement of shoulder-in on four tracks will not cause any horse to sacrifice his balance to the detriment of the forehand.

What, therefore, is the origin, the reasoning, behind the rule of three tracks? It is, once again, plainly and simply the pulling and dragging on the reins because, an unschooled horse who is prevented from running forward and put into the position of shoulder-in by the force of the reins will, without question, run onto the forehand. The negative effect of this grave riding error increases as the angle of the movement increases.

Rein pressure will make the horse fall on the forehand anyway but, if the angle is increased, then the hind legs have to cross more strongly, which means stepping sideways. If this happens, even with the best will in the world, the horse cannot compensate for the rein pressure any more and must burden the forehand – so strongly that it is obvious even to the judges and rule makers.

Thus a grave riding error has evolved into a nonsensical rule that, unopposed, is practised everywhere. If I release the reins and give the aids for the basic collection of the haunches, then I can 'tie the horse's legs into knots' and he will not fall on the forehand. What happens in shoulder-in? The greater the angle of the horse, the more the character of the movement changes from being only a movement of collection to one that is also suppling and very gymnasticizing. In the first case, the inner hind leg must step very far under the centre of gravity of the horse's body. In the second case the horse must cross his legs very strongly. Which is to be done?

If we approach learning shoulder-in the way it has been described in this book, then the degree of angle is relatively uninteresting in the early stages. The main thing is that the horse realizes what we want from him, crosses exactly and promptly, and follows our requests without mechanical aids. If we do not disturb the horse in any way then he can never do anything wrong, because he uses his natural way of going and his fine in-born sense of balance at every moment. The reins must not pull him into position. That is one of the reasons why I hardly ever get near a horse with mechanical aids. To do so, I must have a very compelling reason because I am challenging nature and must take full responsibility for the consequences!

Only when the horse has understood the basic idea of the movement can I begin to think about small differences in the degree of the angle. Depending on the horse, the level of schooling and the demands of the current exercise, I will vary the angle of the shoulder-in between three and four tracks depending on whether I want more collection, carrying-power, forward pushing or a more suppling, gymnasticizing effect.

How to decide which to use is not something that can be learnt from a book; feel and intuition must be brought into play. Then you will always be able to recognize these subtle nuances and increasingly be able to incorporate them into the ever more precise work. So, for goodness sake, do not be afraid of the fourth track.

The dance begins: the change through the circle at liberty

Everywhere in France, Spain, and Portugal you can see this: at a small signal from a horseman holding a lunge line the horse turns instantly to be worked in the opposite direction. In most cases though, the horse simply turns on the haunches. The turns only gymnasticize the horse when he does a clean change of direction through the circle. Not only is this exercise beautiful to look at, not only does it enrich and vary the work in the picadero, but it is also a way to bend the horse and bring him into collected balance without the lunge line.

The illustration on page 131 shows the pattern the horse must describe. Here again, proceed very slowly and be careful not to turn something very meaningful into a cheap trick to show off what the horse can do.

Such a tight bend through the circle is

By this stage, communicatio with the horse is by barely perceptible signals. This change through the circle greatly gymnasticizes the horse because he must bend himself according to the arc of the circle, step well unde and always maintain his balance.

In the first photo we see that I have moved my left shoulder back slightly as well as my left leg and, mos

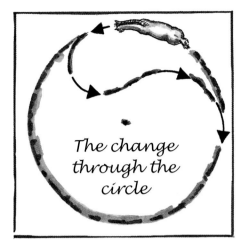

The change through the circle

very strenuous for the horse and he must accustom himself to it gradually. Later on, even when he masters this change at a canter, we will turn him only **once, or a maximum of five times**, during a lunge session. A horse's life is long, especially when we work with him meaningfully and sensibly. Proceed slowly, do not rush anything, do not overdo anything. Here, as in so many areas, less is more.

As easy as this exercise looks, as easy as it basically is, you and your horse will need some time before you can perform it correctly and fluidly.

bviously, the hip. The horse ses this phase to collect imself, step under more trongly, and prepare himself or the forthcoming tight urn.

In the second photo, the orse is in the turn exactly nd evenly bent. The osition of my body is such hat the horse can easily pass ne. The stallion does this xpressively, playfully and in he spirit of showing off.

First the principle, i.e. the individual dance steps. You hold the short whip and the lunge crossed in one hand as the illustration (right) shows. In this illustration the horse is moving to the left.

Now, three things occur simultaneously, each individual move is very simple but, when they are done properly together, it becomes a rather complex matter. First the horseman leaves his small circle in order to step a bit further toward the head of the horse and to create enough room for the horse to be able to change through the circle unhindered (1). At the same time the horseman clearly and emphatically cocks his hip backward. The horse will understand this as an invitation and will respond as desired.

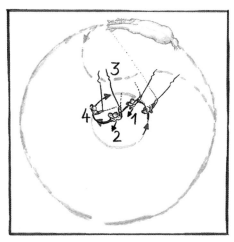

The change through the circle - the path of the horseman

The photos on pages 134–141 clarify this point.

On this particular afternoon Doris, who kindly assumed the role of horse for these pictures was being totally silly, to Birgit's great amusement. What is important, however, is the manner in which Birgit is holding the lunge line and whip in one hand. The lunge line is running between the index and middle finger. The whip is held in the same hand between thumb and index finger. The other hand holds the excess line. In this way the lunge line can be easily lengthened or shortened.

So, the leading hand has to perform two tasks. First it has to maintain the gentle connection to the horse through the lunge line and, second, it must subtly, lightly master the whip as a signal instrument. In the second photo we can see that very well. Birgit holds the whip where the horse's croup would be. Because Doris has only two legs, Birgit must see the rest of the horse in her mind's eye. Practice the correct holding of the whip and lunge line, as well as the following sequence of movements, with a human friend first.

The next four photos show the use of the whip through a correctly executed change. Birgit moves on the small circle, whip in correct position. In the same moment that she makes room at the mid-point, she cocks her hip backward and lifts the whip over the 'horse' in order to create a visible barricade.

Next, still in this same phase of the movement, the lunge whip is lifted over the horse (3) so that while you are in your new position in front of your horse it acts as a boundary.

These three elements together, which should be done in a very fluid, dancelike way, are sufficiently clear signals to enable the horse to change through the circle in the desired manner without any pull on the lunge line (2).

The horse will now pass by the horseman, who must stand still in this phase (4). It is not correct to give way to the horse. The natural willingness of the horse to yield to an 'authority figure' has been so developed by this point that the quietly standing horseman is a signal to the horse that he should keep an appropriate distance while passing. Once this has happened the horseman immediately turns back onto his small circle in order to take up the basic triangle position again. That completes the exercise.

Always practise without the horse initially. A human assistant can be very helpful as we study and practise the required movement sequences until they become almost automatic.

When everything becomes harmonious, ask someone who knows absolutely nothing about all this to be the 'horse'. Ask them to respond to your signals, gestures, and movements as they believe they should be interpreted. If you do everything correctly, your 'ignorant' helper will react absolutely correctly and, in the next phase, so will your horse.

Once you have your four-legged friend on the lunge, project peace, complete authority and endless patience; you cannot have enough of that.

As always, you begin in walk. To make sure your horse truly changes through the circle rather than simply making a turn on the haunches (which, as a rule, always happens in the very beginning), it is important to make your gestures particularly clear, emphatic and precise and, in the early stages, to back up a fair distance to really open up the centre of the picadero. You virtually have to show the horse the way to go with your gestures and your body.

However your horse reacts, even if he only gives you a little of what you requested, praise him and move on to another exercise.

Increasingly, the horse will realize what you want of him and eventually he will change through the circle at trot and later even at canter.

The photos on pages 134–141 will make all this clear.

Since we have moved into areas which demand a fairly high level of 'feel', empathy, and sensitivity, I would like to give you an example of something which, at first glance, might not seem to belong here, but it has tremendous relevance to working with that magnificent being, the horse.

About laughing eyes and crying eyes

In the illustration below we see two faces, one laughing, the other crying. What is so special about this? At first glance, probably nothing. But, if we look at the eyes of the first face, are they not laughing? And are the eyes on the face on the right not crying?

Does not everything about the face on the left seem to be laughing and everything about the face on the right seem to be sad? Is a circle always a circle – a person a person – a horse a horse? No, not always! This example from gestalt psychology tells us something different, that is that every visible element is in truth a carrier of an emotional quality! A circle is just a circle – circumference, diameter, radius – yet sometimes it seems to be crying and other times it is laughing, without any change in its basic circular form.

What this example illustrates happens in every respect and circumstance though we are, as a rule, unaware of its effect on us for good or ill. But a horse reacts almost exclusively to these subtle emotional messages. To the horse, a person is not simply a person, a conception of a being, but much more; he is the emotional quality that he projects through his entire being, the totality of his movements and gestures. To the horse we are nothing more than a simple circle that, without visibly changing its circular form signals laughing one time, crying another, and so much more too. The horse reacts accordingly: once one way, and another time in exactly the opposite fashion.

The deeper we wish to explore the horse – and all life – the more we should try to sharpen our perception of the world of emotional differentiation behind the visible foreground. The horse's world and all his experiences lie in the world of the senses to which our technical civilization can offer nothing but right angles, norms, and formulas.

This picture shows how the whip is held during work. The right hand holds the whip and the lunge line, the left hand takes up the excess line in order to subtly lengthen or shorten it.

The simple way of holding the whip

ere we see a sequence
nowing the simple way of
olding the whip, which we
ue in the early phases: the
ght hand holds both the
nge line and the whip. The
hip gives occasional sup-
orting signals.

In the second photo I
repare for the change.
he most important signal
or this is cocking the hip
ackward. At that point the
hip is still behind the
orse.

In the next photo, the
orse has begun the turn. My
ip is well back and the
hip is lifted, ready to be
oved over the horse. The
nge line remains softly
oped in all phases. The
ourth photo shows the
ccessful change. The whip
as been moved to the left,
ow to be held again in the
asic position.

The whip in one hand

On these two pages we see a perfect sequence of two changes and a halt. The whip is held in a simple basic position. It can only be employed when the human as well as the horse has mastered the exercise.

In the second photo the locked-back hip signals the turn. The horse seems to be interested in something in the distance but, nevertheless, goes willingly into the turn, although not correctly bent and positioned.

The transition from one direction to the other is not so simple for the horseman as he must get back into the basic triangle position very quickly.

Pictures three and four show that although my steps are smaller they are nevertheless still *going*

forward! This is most important. In this position it is easy to yield to the oncoming horse; at the beginning that always happens but it is fundamentally incorrect! Back on the circle, photo six shows the introduction of the second change of direction. The horse follows willingly. Stepping under very nicely, he is attentive and also in the correct position. Again I am going slowly *forward* and very quickly arrive again in the correct basic position. With quiet, regular steps I accompany the horse on my small circle and then, with an emphatic short signal I bring the horse to a beautiful halt. Praise, two treats and off into his stall or stable or out to his paddock he goes.

The free horse

This exercise, the change through the circle, is one of the most beautiful of the groundwork exercises but at the same time also one of the most difficult, so, I would like to show and explain to you once more the individual phases, which Birgit and Janosch have so wonderfully executed.

Birgit performed the exercise in a large paddock and, thanks to her very clear and precise body language, she was successful at keeping the horse attentive to her even at great distances. Let us look at each individual stage of how she accomplished this.

In the first photo we see how Birgit 'leads' the horse with the left hand. She describes exactly the arc the horse subsequently makes. In the second photo we see the hip cocked backward. The horse positions himself wonderfully, steps deeply under himself, and changes direction as desired. His

xpression is attentive and e is focussed on Birgit as he asses her in the change and mmediately establishes imself on a tight volte, gain in a beautiful position photos four, five and six). he horse is correctly ositioned and bent. lthough he is some distance way from Birgit, he is, ttentive and working with her. With a dancelike movement Birgit signals another change, which he promptly and willingly performs (photos seven, eight and nine).

See how wonderfully the hand, hip and whip work together to lead the horse into the new change. These are the exercises that, in an unbelievably effective way, school and gymnasticize a horse, making him supple, and taking him further and further into equilibrium and self-carriage. Note how the horse works with joy, attentiveness, and enthusiasm. No pulling and dragging is necessary, no threatening raising of the whip, it is simply pleasure and play with horse and human in true harmony.

(Photos on pages 140 and 141.) Like a toreador with a bull, Birgit plays beautifully and elegantly with the horse. With her body she brings the horse into a tight turn. The horse whooshes by her, very close, almost wrapping himself around her. Through all of this the horse is beautifully positioned even

in the smallest, tightest turns. Finally, as Birgit gives the horse a short halt signal, the horse stands and gratefully and joyfully accepts the praise he has so thoroughly earned.

Working with horses in this way is *not* written about in books. Janosch is truly not an easy horse. For years he violently resisted subordinating himself to humans and being ridden but today he is one of the most dependable partners imaginable, a being who feels himself understood, respected and, above all, listened to. He gets an unending flow of gratification, not from having a Christmas wreath in his stall or a gold trimmed rug, but from humans who interact with him like friends.

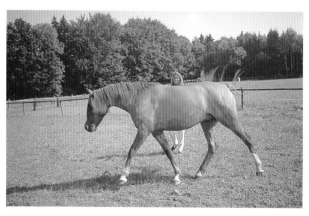

The principles of communication through body language allow themselves to be carried over to riding very simply. If you continue to observe the rules, you realize very quickly that, whether for flexing the horse, bending him, or putting him into a correct position, the mechanical use of the reins is *not* necessary.

The photo shows that, at this moment, my weight is shifted to the inside, with the horse's movement. A simple but very precise turn of my upper body sends the horse eight different pieces of information (*see* pages 156–157) : aids, which really are 'aids', but which are so soft and gentle that they remain invisible.

Riding
The Ground Rules for Collected, Body-controlled Riding with Weight Aids

When I sit on a horse, I become over 2.3 m (7 ft 6 in) tall at the shoulders. At this height every movement, even if it is only a few millimetres, affects the equilibrium of the horse almost like a landslide! Should not that amount of power be sufficient to communicate with the being beneath me?

Again, is everything different?

Now the time has come for us to sit on the horse, to ride. I intend to continue to justify and show the reasoning behind everything I say. It is not about accepting and believing something untried on trust alone. My intention is to describe things in such a way that they become understandable and can be logically followed and carried out because only understanding makes it possible to develop your own point of view and to independently and creatively put it into practice.

I have the impression that, in the horse world (and not only there) far too much of what is done is unproven, accepted on trust and practised unquestioningly and uncritically. 'Don't question so much – it has always been done like this!' But has it really? Is not much of what is currently practised and passed on under the mantle of tradition in truth of fairly recent development? Are these not customs and habits which, for the most part, originated only in the twentieth century?

I do not use a throatlatch, nor do I ride in a 20 x 60 m arena, nor do I always mount on the left and never facing toward the croup. Those are all habits, among so many others, which have made themselves at home among us. That is not to say that they are necessarily bad, but should not each of us at least know why we are doing something one way and not another? In my lectures and demonstrations I always question these common practices and the reasons for them. To date, I have received virtually no answers.

Let us take the throatlatch as an example. This thing has to be cut to the right length, sewn, attached and then cared for. Everyone seems to know that a throatlatch should always be buckled fairly loosely. But what in the world is the purpose of it? And why in the world does no one ask about it? The background is so simple it is almost laughable. The throatlatch comes, as does so much else, from military riding. Horses were considered war supplies and were treated accordingly. After many days marching it often happened that a horse, even the most willing, was no longer able to carry his rider. The rider then was forced to dismount and pull his horse along! So that the bridle would not slip off, the throatlatch was tightly buckled on.

I have never met a rider who, these days, drags his horse around the arena or across the countryside in this manner. Nonetheless, every bridle is equipped with a throatlatch, an absolutely superfluous and even bothersome piece of equipment.

The list of questionable practices could be very long indeed, but I do not want to continue it here. I would, however, just like to ask you to question the practices I show you here and to prove their logic for yourself. Everything I have described has an explainable, understandable background. It is my belief that only he who can give sensible reasons and solid proof for what he says and does deserves to be believed and trusted.

The 'Sunday afternoon passage in bedroom slippers'. If you are to do without the reins as they are commonly employed even to High School level, then you must follow a clear, simple system that is distinguished from the commonly known one solely by its simplicity. The truth is always very simple – unfortunately much too simple for most human beings.

The five pillars of riding

the bend of the horse in the
volte. After halting, turning
is the most important
challenge of riding. I still
remember my early days
as a rider which were
characterized by my going to
every possible practitioner of
every conceivable style of
riding in order to ask, 'How
do you ride the turn?' I got
exactly as many answers as
the number of people of
whom I asked the question.

The explanation of the
English-riding group struck
me as the least sensible. 'You
must position the horse with
the reins, but then the horse
will escape at the croup [the
horse's hindquarters will
escape] so the outside leg
must be placed a long way
back to prevent this. The pull
of the reins will make the
horse spiral to the centre, so
you must use your inside leg
to push him out'. Sure.
Anything else?

At the beginning of this book I stated that
riding is very simple. This is a very daring
statement in light of the many thick books
on the subject and in light of the difficulties so many people have with riding. I
said that because riding is among the most
natural processes of all and therefore **simple enough for anyone to accomplish**.
However, if I ignore the natural nature of
a process, then it really does become complicated.

Again and again I demonstrate with
young horses that they will position
themselves perfectly in a volte without
bit or bridle and, so, logically, without
being pulled into the movement with the
reins.

If you go to a standing horse and tug
on his halter or bridle, his hindquarters
will automatically turn in the opposite
direction. This response is even more
obvious when the horse is in motion. If I
guide my horse into the volte by pulling
on the reins the haunches must necessar-

ily fall out: it is a simple compensation, a
purely natural reaction. So this is where
riding begins to get complicated because
now the bend must be determined by
the outside leg etc., in order to achieve
what the horse would have done on his
own if he had been left to himself. One
of the most natural processes in the
world – a horse turning – becomes a
complicated act of riding accompanied
by technical finesse and a thousand
tricks.

If we view riding as a natural process,
something which children, as already
mentioned, intuitively feel, then we discover that the whole can be reduced to
five points.

1. Movement compensation
2. Balance and seat
3. Change of direction
4. Change of gait and tempo
5. Collection

1. Movement compensation

When I happen to visit a horse show there is one thing that repeatedly puzzles me: how, with all that bouncing in the saddle, do the hats stay on? And, I ask myself: can that be fun, to be shaken and rattled around like that? Interestingly enough, the exercise is called 'sitting'. Does that mean that the hat sits?

There 'sits' a rider, stiff as a board on a moving force, meaning the hips are completely rigid. Everything else – thighs, calves, upper back, shoulders and head – is naturally moving quite forcefully.

Giving subtle, sensitive aids via a slight body signal is impossible in that situation. The rider is forced to communicate with the reins and other more or less rough means. There can be no talk of a true connection between horse and human, because that comes into being only when the rider absorbs, or compensates for, with his own body, the movement offered by the horse.

In walk and trot the lifting and lowering of the hind legs is associated with a very specific movement of the back. Let us stay with trot. The diagonal fore and hind legs move off and land at the same time. Because of that, a slight wave-like dynamic forward motion occurs which has its greatest force at the moment of moving off. In the suspension phase the momentum drops off a little only to have renewed power when the next diagonal pair move off.

By moving off the horse develops not only pushing power but also power thrusting upward; this is very different, as can be easily demonstrated with a trampoline. If you move in a way that imitates the way your horse moves his hind legs at the trot, and your body is without tension, you will prove to yourself that your hips move in exactly the opposite direction to your legs. If the left leg goes up, the left hip drops. If the right leg lifts, the right hip sinks down. You will observe exactly the same thing in your horse when he is trotting. So the upward movement of the horse is not a consistent up-and-down, but more a swinging movement right to left that carries into the saddle area.

The upper body of a rider on a normal-sized horse is at a height of 1.6–2.6 m (5 ft 3 in–8 ft 8 in) at shoulder height. Imagine yourself carrying a person on your shoulders at this height. You will feel every slight shift of weight from above very clearly, and you will also most likely find

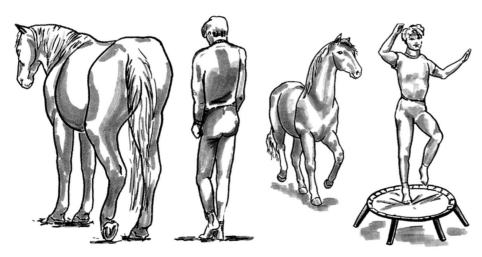

it very uncomfortable. If you begin to move, each shift of weight will have a much greater effect. You will have to make a great effort to maintain your own balance and move forward with any degree of regularity.

The situation is exactly the same for the horse. Every shift of the rider's weight will be noticeable as an extreme disturbance of the horse's already fragile balance.

If, in addition, a rider wants to use the individual parts of his body separately to give subtle and unequivocal signals to his horse, it follows logically that: **the rider should find his way into the movement of the horse in such a way that the individual parts of his body appear to be still within the forward motion.** Only in that way is it possible to use subtle and specific body signals.

Learn to sit in one hour?

Sitting a horse seems to be one of the most complicated parts of riding – at least that is the impression given by riding schools and riding students. I maintain that a person with a body of normal mobility can learn to sit a horse in one to three hours on the lunge line, especially if they are an absolute beginner at riding.

It is important though that the biomechanics of the horse in all gaits have first been made understandable to the rider. 'Made understandable' means that he can see the movement mechanics, that he understands the individual sequences and that he can, with closed eyes, feel the movement and find his way into it.

I will now try to explain this step by step and for this I will stay with the most difficult gait, the trot. For this purpose the human body is mentally divided into three parts. There is the upper body, down to the navel, the seat, including the pelvis and hips, and, finally, the legs.

In the piaffe the rider feels clearly the left/right tipping movement of the horse and the rider's pelvis executes basically the same movement that it does in walk. In the normal trot movement the forward push is added to this so that the pelvis makes a semi-circular movement.

Before you sit on a horse for the first time, you should be clear about the mechanics of the horse's movement. If you then feel what you have studied by experimenting a bit with these movements, then neither sitting the trot nor following the movement of the canter should be a problem. Here in the piaffe we see how the left hip sinks as the left leg starts its stride. With the upward movement of the right foreleg the right shoulder moves upward too. The whole horse is now higher on the right side than on the left. He is rocking and that 'oh so complicated' sitting is nothing more than following this left/right, or right/left, rocking with the pelvis.

The rider's calves and thighs are extraordinarily important information-conveying aids which, through correct and consistent positioning can transmit the most subtle signals. A continuous bracing and springing in the stirrups as is recommended in so many text books leads to inconvenient cramping and tensing of the leg muscles and of course to continuous superfluous activity which makes giving subtle signals impossible.

The legs are not capable of catching the upward and forward movement of the horse. The pelvis and the upper body are connected with each other through the spine. This is extraordinarily mobile and can be made significantly more so through the appropriate gymnastic exercises. It is in this area of the body that movement compensation can be undertaken. The immobile upper body serves as a signal giver and, for this reason, the pelvis and the lower part of the spine (to the level of the navel) compensate for the forward and upward movement of the horse. This

means that, in every gait, the legs and upper body appear to be absolutely still and not to change within the total movement. The pelvis finds itself passive in the wave-like movement of the horse so that a continuous connection with the horse's back is possible, with no disruption.

Riding is like running, walking and jumping; the same rules apply. The hips, pelvis and parts of the spine, with the supporting push, pull, and hold powers of the muscles, compensate for the pushing and lifting powers of the legs. Riding is, therefore, just as easy as going for a walk, but both must be practised.

If the rider masters this fairly simple foundation then no longer will the stress of the horse's movement travel to the upper body. All the elements of the horse's motion are absorbed and equalized below the navel.

Now signal headquarters, the body, is in the perfect position. The legs lie absolutely quietly and delicately on the sides of the horse. Every least change in the position

In the passage the 'rocking and upward movement' of the horse is felt much more strongly. Here you can see more clearly than in the photo of the piaffe the side to side movement of the horse. The whole left side is higher than the right. In passage the rider must soften the right/left movement with his pelvis and absorb it through the appropriate sideways dropping and lifting if he does not want to be thrown off.

Once again we see passage, this time without a saddle. The horse's right shoulder is lifted and, my left knee, just like my left hip, is lower than the right. My shoulders, on the other hand are level. That is the principle of movement compensation in trot. The upper body is still, the shoulders are always level with no unintentional shifting. The pelvis goes passively into the right/left movement of the horse. Because of that, the legs too appear to be still because they remain in the same place and only move with the movement of the horse's side. They lie gently and quietly on the horse's belly and passively allow themselves to be taken along for the ride.

or pressure of one or both legs can now clearly be interpreted by the horse as a signal.

The upper body appears to be an absolutely still pole from which the horse appears to be hung. Now the rider is no longer disturbing the horse's balance. On the contrary, through his quiet and consistent presence he 'catches' irregularities and balances them out. This is very important, and not just with young horses.

The pelvis unites itself with the movement presented by the horse and so 'melts' into the horse's back to become as one with it.

If this harmony is interrupted, it will be instantly perceived by the horse and, if he has had appropriate schooling, be interpreted as a signal and translated into action. Practised in this way, riding in all gaits is not only extraordinarily comfortable but, above all, extraordinarily healthy. Through the continual soft movement of the abdominal area the most important vital organs of the rider are being constantly massaged. Not a single hard bump penetrates the body to eventually damage the spine. That sort of damage is exactly what happens when the pelvis does not compensate for the horse's movement and the rider is bounced out of the saddle with every step. Then riding is a very risky undertaking for both man and horse.

Sitting passively in the movement

The additional weight, the burden of the rider, becomes detrimental to the horse if his balance and the rhythm of his movement are disturbed. It is these disturbances that, as a rule, create the health problems, the injuries and the wear and tear on the horse's body. Once the balance is re-established under the weight of a rider, and if that rider is no longer disrupting the horse's rhythm of movement, then the additional weight is no longer a problem for the horse. The demand on the rider is that, in every movement he must **find his way into, and sit in, the movement** of the horse. He must find the common centre of gravity with the horse and passively go along with the rhythm of the movement.

It is finding this 'oneness' with the movement of the horse that is so very meaningful. Again and again I see attempts to 'drive' horses, that is to push them forward with the pelvis, or the seat. Aside from the fact that because of this the horse becomes ever duller and can only be ridden with ever greater expenditures of energy, through this strong intervention in

the rhythm of the movement, both the horse's balance and his natural rhythm are being continually disturbed.

Never should a horse be rhythmically driven to a quicker pace, either with the legs or with the seat.

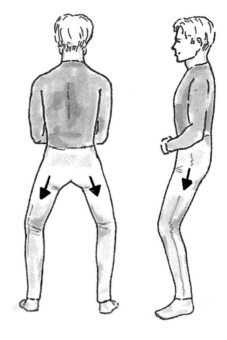

Walk

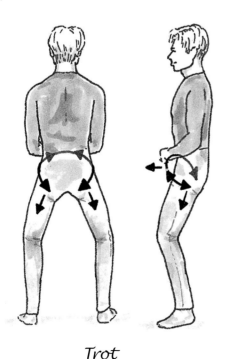

Trot

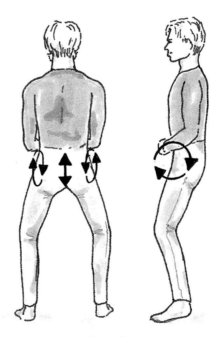

Canter

The entire sequence of movement on a horse is comparable to the natural walking and running movements of humans. Here too the lifting and placing of the feet is translated into flowing forward movement through the swing of the pelvis.

In handicapped riding programmes handicapped people are given the opportunity to rediscover the natural pelvic movement of walking by finding their way into (following) the movement of the horse.

When riding and when giving aids while riding we find that exactly the same rules apply to the forward movement of humans. For this reason riding is such a natural and intuitive activity and above all a process of **feeling and transferring**.

'Tell me again the aids for a turn on the haunches. I've forgotten them.' That, or something similar, is something I am frequently asked during riding lessons. And my answer? 'Please do a turn on the haunches yourself, without the horse, and then you'll have no difficulty feeling the correct aids.'

Imagine that your left leg is the left hind leg of the horse. To be able to do a 'turn on the haunches' you must first burden the leg to the left. To do this you will shift your entire body weight to the left keeping the spine vertical, the shoulders level and in line with the hips, and not collapsing either the waist or the hips, i.e. keeping the body parallel to the position from which you have just shifted. In addition your upper body will move very slightly backward. In order to turn, your upper body will automatically turn slightly to the left into the movement and your right leg will come forward. In this way you have stabilized your body in such a way that you can safely and comfortably execute a 'turn on the haunches'.

And this is just what we will carry over in giving the aids to our horse, who must carry himself, who will carry himself, the same way.

By passively going forward, by passively following his movement, we are providing the horse with a disturbance-free and balanced flow of movement that is interrupted when we give a short, subtle, but nevertheless emphatic, aid. The horse will respond instantly in order to re-establish the disturbance-free flow of movement. Once this occurs, the rider immediately returns to passively following the movement of the horse. The prerequisite for this is the harmonious melting together of rider and horse into one movement!.

This process is an essential part of riding and, as we shall see later, this point of connection between human and horse, the seat, is, the most important channel for effective communication. That means, of course, that a certain suppleness, is necessary in the lower part of the spine.

In the beginning it is necessary to lightly round the whole spine in order to truly meet the requirement of sitting passively in the movement. From such a rounded-back seat comes, without force or false ambition, the seat which is aesthetically pleasing, comfortable and, above all, very precise in transmitting aids.

As you are riding circles in the picadero, every once in a while think of something completely different. Play ball with your free hands, listen to music; just turn your little grey brain cells in a completely different direction and give your body a chance to find the natural rhythm.

In our first lessons on the horse we will attempt to put this into practice, to find our way into and follow the movement of the horse. And, as said, it is not as difficult as is commonly believed, if you are prepared to feel, to let yourself fall, and if you are prepared to give up the permanently active role and passively allow yourself to be carried.

2. Balance and seat

We have already said quite a lot about the importance of balance. The way we sit on a horse determines whether we will find this common balance or totally destroy it.

In the twentieth century particularly, styles of riding came into fashion which are greatly removed from the nature of riding and from the natural style of riding. Modern equestrian sport and modern sport-horse breeding are responsible for this.

When a physically healthy person sits on an unsaddled horse, he will, completely automatically, assume a typical position that is always the same: his upper body will incline slightly backward and his back will be lightly rounded. The pelvis is slightly tilted, and the legs hang long, stretched downward, on the horse's belly.

This is the most natural and the only correct position for sitting on a horse. The pelvis and back can absorb the movement of the horse and at the same time influence and control the hindquarters. Because of the free movement of the pelvis, any bumping and pounding of the horse is not carried over into the rider's upper body. This can, in a firm but released position, quietly control the movement and balance of the horse. Because the rider is sitting fairly far back on the horse, his legs also lie well back and can, with very minimal signals, activate and influence the haunches.

Nature and the naturalness of the movements give us everything. There is no reason to change anything about this.

The saddles we use, therefore, should be so constructed that they do not change anything about this basic position and, in addition, they should make possible the most intimate contact with the horse. Franco-Iberian saddles generally tend to satisfy these requirements. From France we have the Carmargue saddle, which has

When a person, preferably one with no riding experience, sits on an unsaddled horse, he will automatically assume a particular position. The most obvious thing (and we can see this in the first photo below) is that the legs hang long, practically straight, on the horse's side, and evenly, gently wrap around the horse's belly. In addition, you see that the rider sits comparatively far back, that her pelvis is tilted slightly forward (this can be seen in the second photo) and that the upper body is slightly behind the vertical with the back lightly rounded. As a rule, the total picture gives an impression of relaxation and also of beauty and elegance.

Sitting on a horse is not something that has to be learnt; it is an anatomically logical and natural position.

Birgit sometimes tends to sit in the saddle with a slightly hollowed back. Even here in the basic position on the ground you can see this tendency. The seat is pushed backward, the navel comes forward and the back is hollow. In this position it is almost impossible to compensate for the movement of the horse. Many riders have this same difficulty. Continually check yourself at home in front of a mirror and make an effort to find the correct basic position with a straight, or very slightly rounded, back.

been built the same way for centuries. It is especially suited for small compact horses with short powerful backs. If you own such a horse, you must try such a saddle.

In Spain and Portugal we find the most differently made dressage saddles and the widest variety of them. As a rule these saddles are of somewhat lighter construction than other saddles and are intended for the High School exercises. The Spanish *vaquero*, or bullfighting, saddle, on the other hand, is larger and heavier and with its fleece covered seat is suited for long rides. One thing all these saddles have in common is that they put the rider's centre of gravity backward and also permit a natural deep seat, particularly for the untrained rider. A number of Western saddles also meet these requirements, although most of them are too heavy and too large. Many Texas-made saddles make it virtually impossible for the rider to put his legs in the correct position and let them hang softly against the horse's belly. Old saddles of the California style, on the other hand, are often very usable. Now and then you find good saddles from South America, most are hybrids of Spanish and American saddles. As a rule, the Western saddles from South America are not only lighter and less expensive (but just as good quality), they also put the rider in a better position.

Here we see a Spanish shepherd's saddle. It is made almost exclusively of straw or a particular reed, which molds itself perfectly to the horse's back and the rider's seat when the saddle is ridden-in. It is extraordinarily comfortable and places the rider's centre of gravity well back.

With a new saddle like this one, the fleece, which is put over the saddle body for protection, is still thick and plush and therefore has the disadvantage of forcing the rider's legs forward and off the horse's body. Such a saddle only shows its true worth and quality at about the time when a civilized middle-European would disgustedly wrinkle his nose at that 'broken old thing'.

Top   These saddles from southern France are my favourites, though, unfortunately, for many reasons they can only be used for horses up to 150 cm (14.3 hh) tall. The built-up pommel and cantle are not there just to ensure that a drunken rider gets home safely, rather, they are intended for work with steers. Hardly any saddle has such an advantageous centre of gravity as this one, and hardly any other saddle comes as close to the natural bareback seat of a rider as this one.

Middle   Seen historically, Western riding is derived from the Iberian style of riding. Simplification and modification increase as you travel further north in America. A Western saddle like the one shown here, modeled on a Texan saddle, has, in my opinion, the disadvantage of placing the rider comparatively far forward, and, it is built on such a massive tree that the rider's legs are forced off the sides of the horse. Saddles of the California design are much more similar to the Spanish ones and therefore are, as a rule, more useful.

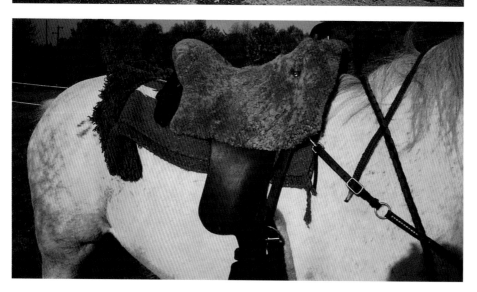

Bottom   Here we see a fleece-covered South American saddle which was not constructed for gaited horses. Such saddles are still very close to the Spanish originals and most are very usable and often much less expensive than comparable Western saddles. The centre of gravity is well back and the construction of the saddle allows a soft draping of the rider's legs.

Here we see Claudia in the saddle shown at the bottom of page 154. You can see how the saddle helps the rider find a natural seat.

With luck, you can also find good saddles of German manufacture. There are the 'Trachtensattel', endurance saddles and saddles made on the pattern of the old military saddles, which are all thoroughly usable. The deciding factor is whether the saddle fills the requirements we have already mentioned and allows for a natural, relaxed seat.

All the so-called 'English' dressage and sport saddles which are so commonly available are absolutely unusable. In my opinion they are a physiological catastrophe and run counter to every law of natural riding!

Most probably you cannot or will not want to do without such a saddle if you are the owner of a tall and long horse. In that case it might actually be necessary to work carefully in a light seat with such a saddle in the very beginning and then, after appropriate suppling and strengthening through work in-hand and on the ground, return to traditional, horse-oriented tack.

Please study the photos on page 158 very carefully to develop your eye for a natural 'released' seat, for its suppleness, its comfort, and its effectiveness.

Spanish or Portuguese dressage saddles are designed for a natural riding style but they have a small drawback in that they do not place the rider back far enough. Therefore, they are intended for horses already fairly far advanced in their training. The rider, too, should possess a good and established seat.

3. Balance and change of direction

Consciously walk a 5 m (16 ft 6 in) circle. What are you doing exactly? How does it feel when you examine it more closely? First you will turn your head in the direction you are going, to the left in this example. At the same time your shoulders and hips will turn. You have shifted your weight slightly to the inside so that your left leg is slightly more burdened and so that you can remain stable as you walk on the curve of the circle.

Why should it work any differently on horseback? Why should I 'turn the horse's head with the reins', 'wrap him around my inner leg' and 'keep his haunches on the circle with the outside calf' which is pulled back so far it is nearly horizontal, when my nature and my intuition are telling me something completely different?

In fact, one single movement is enough to give my horse eight pieces of information (see below) so that he can correctly and in accordance with his nature execute turns and voltes, with expression, power and brilliance.

A simple and correct rotation of the rider's body, as shown in the photo on page 157 (and which is invisible when the rider is on horseback since the horse follows the turn), gives my four-legged partner the following eight-point information.

1. The turn of my head and the direction of my gaze 'announce' the direction of the turn. My horse perceives this as valuable information.
2. The turning of the whole upper body signals the degree of the desired change of direction. That, too, is information required by the horse.
3. The rotation of the upper body also turns the pelvis. This gives very clear and precise information that helps the horse take a correct position and bend.

4. With the rotation of the torso and the pelvis, in this case to the left, the right leg will lie more strongly on the horse, thereby, without changing its position, holding the horse steady in the turn.
5. With the rotation of the upper body to the left, the rider's inner (left) leg, will be imperceptibly taken away from the horse's side. Because a horse, by his nature, yields to pressure and this tendency becomes ever more refined in the course of schooling, this slight movement of the inside leg allows him to yield more easily to the increased pressure of the outside leg.

In order to understand the phenomenon of riding around a corner or bend, I ask that participants in my courses consciously perform a turn, or try a half-pass (bottom photo) on foot. The relevant feelings and movements can be carried over to riding 100 per cent because, as riders, we merely borrow the legs of the horse.

In the first photo Gisela shows us how to 'ride' a perfect volte. Naturally, I did not tell her that; she is doing nothing more than walking in a circle. And that is exactly how we ride a perfect volte! But, what is she doing? She is looking in the direction in which she is travelling which is very important. Her upper body is turned in the correct direction and consequently her pelvis is also turned. Her shoulders are exactly level and, most importantly, her body weight is distinctly shifted to the inside – the upper body has, so to speak, made a parallel displacement to the inside. You cannot ride a volte on the horse more exactly than that. Once again: riding is very simple. If only people would believe that.

Here you see me in a dry run of 'riding a turn'; I am greatly exaggerating the individual movements and shifts of weight in order to make them visible. The total coordination when on horseback is so very fine, but also so very clear and influential, that this simple turning is enough to transmit very precise information to the horse, invisible to any observer. The totality of the information transmitted allows itself to be broken down into eight individual pieces.

This small movement correctly, precisely and invisibly executed on horseback is the foundation of classical Franco-Iberian riding with weight aids! It is the alpha and the omega of sensitive, natural horse-oriented riding. The basics of the movement are the same movements made by a person walking on foot. The horse follows the rotation of the upper body, constantly working to conform to, by correct movement, the precise 'imbalance' deliberately presented by the rider.

6. At first, when the rider is still 'steering' with the loose reins, with two hands, the rotation of the upper body will cause the inside rein to be very slightly taken up, without becoming taut, simply because the rider's hands follow the body in the turn.

7. Through the rotation of the upper body the outside rein will automatically lie on the neck of the horse, who will become evermore sensitive to this signal.

8. A very significant final point: in a correctly executed rotation of the upper body the rider's weight will shift. In order to re-establish the balance, the horse will automatically and instinc-

tively step under the rider's weight. In our example he will move left.

In fact, hidden in this method of riding turns and circles is a big part of the secret of riding overall. When these things are done correctly, all further, increasingly difficult exercises, even to High School level can be done with amazing ease. Without this essential skill, these exercises can barely be done at all, certainly not with impulsion and brilliance.

Because the rider's legs are always draped softly around the horse's body and do not really change their position forward or backward, and because the horse is able to instantly follow the rotation of the rider's upper body, it is possible to ride even the tightest turns and smallest circles with **absolutely invisible aids**.

This is also the foundation for the all-important shoulder-in, which can also be executed with fine, totally invisible, shifts of weight. The prerequisite for this is the harmonious connection with the horse's back, i.e. truly becoming part of the movement.

I would like to say a few words about the aids for bending the horse around the inside leg as it is commonly taught. In the lessons on leg-yielding, shoulder-in and also half-pass the 'laid-on' leg serves as a signal for the yielding. I think this is a logical and effective way to proceed. In common with the Spanish shepherds and bull-fighters, whose lives often depend on their horses' ability to turn quickly and reliably and in common with many ancient riding cultures, I cannot see why the horse should sometimes yield to the leg aid, and should 'follow' it at other times. I am sorry, I cannot follow that logic. I have found that horses ridden in this way are either pretty confused or dead to the leg since, in the end, the horse is crammed between two legs and is actually led or turned with the reins.

The powerful stepping under of the hind legs is furthered by the unresisting bending of the horse and by the distinct shifting of the rider's weight to the inside which strengthens the influence of the swinging-along inner hip.

By means of these clear, sensitive and sensible aids, the natural talents of the horse are fully revealed and ever more developed and refined. Finally, a very slight rotation of the rider's upper body and a minimal increase in the pressure of the leg are enough to produce the most precise and instantaneous response from the horse.

In the following riding exercises we will concentrate on this point.

Here (top photo) I am doing a demonstration during one of my courses on Petra's Arabian. My gaze and my body determine the direction of movement. My shoulders are level. My inner hip is already weighted, but without collapsing at the waist. My legs are hanging long and straight down the horse's sides, considerably further back, as we can see, than the Western saddle would place them if my feet were in the stirrups. From this position the softly draping legs can wonderfully and subtly affect the haunches of the horse and thus, with minimal signals, collect and position him. The reins hang loose, the horse's posture is good.

A horse trained like this will, in the end, respond instantly to very subtle shifts in the rider's weight but it is necessary for the rider to have a very stable seat, and to be able to keep it consistently so that he is not thrown to the outside by the centrifugal force of the horse's turn. In quick movements, such as this turn on the haunches (2nd photo), that could happen very easily. That would not only hinder the horse in the precise execution of the movement but these are the moments when a horse can injure himself, particularly out in the countryside. It is not just my 80 kg (176 lb) of additional weight (which the horse can easily manage) that causes problems but the fact that now the weight is intensifying and lying mainly on one side thus leading to an unfavourable overburdening of the very delicate legs.

You must imagine that horse and rider are not separated in the middle but are one body, which moves in a stable, unified way. In this

4. Changes in gait and tempo

We have talked about movement compensation in riding, about the passive following of the horse's motion. We have spoken about the seat that evolves from this and the possibilities for changing direction. Now the question remains, how are the gait and tempo of the horse determined, **without disturbing his balance** and without hindering his freedom of movement with mechanical aids?

Anyone who has completed the exercises in this book up to this chapter will be surprised at how he is now able to bring his horse to a complete halt from the ground. The horse responds instantly as though some mechanical force were suddenly intervening. The horse, in a split second, allows himself to be collected, to step under and halt and will hereafter, be more collected, compact, and will carry himself in a more upright posture. He regards us in a kindly way because there has been no pain connected with the exercises. He is responding in accordance with his nature so he is physically and psychically balanced.

We can carry this over to riding but we have to study all the different aspects very precisely and above all differentiate between them.

Changes in gait and tempo

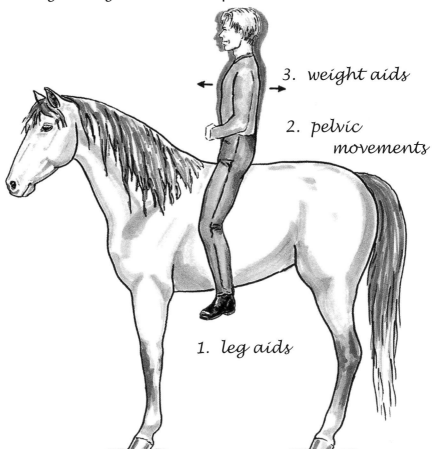

3. *weight aids*

2. *pelvic movements*

1. *leg aids*

photo it can be seen that during the quick movement of the horse, I stay seated with my weight to the inside (left), and so give the horse some help, an 'aid' to do what is asked of him. The word 'aid' is a terrific one – why is it so often misinterpreted?

Here we see Birgit with Sami (centre). She is sitting nice and straight, with level shoulders and she is turned in the direction of the movement. Her weight is to the inside, in his case to the right, and the horse follows it wonderfully and moves in the desired direction.

Birgit allowed me to show you, with the help of the last two photos, what one should *not* do under any circumstances. Here she tries to turn her horse to the left, manages to keep her shoulders at the same height but the inside hip collapses noticeably. When Birgit does this it still looks charming but it is nevertheless totally incorrect because the weight of the rider is now shifted to the outside (the right in this case) and her inside (left) leg is pushing her horse to the right.

In the last photo Birgit shows us a variation of this error. This time she is not only folding or collapsing at the hip/waist but is also letting one shoulder drop. Her right shoulder is visibly lower than the left. Birgit wants to go to the right but, because of her body position, she is sending her horse to the left. In such cases, riders frequently resort to pulling on the inside rein and spurring with the outside leg. Even with the best will in the world the horse cannot go where the rider wants because the rider is pushing him in the opposite direction.

Everything I write in the following pages is based upon my everyday work with horses, the practice of the caballeros and certain bullfighters and, as far as I know, it has never before been written down in this way.

Let us look first at the one thing upon which there is general agreement, namely, that to start or speed-up a horse, as well as to slow him down or halt him, it is necessary to **activate the haunches**.

I activate the haunches by two means.

1. Through the meaningful use of the legs. Sadly, many riders rarely use their legs correctly and meaningfully as, for example, when they drive in rhythm with the gait, i.e. with 'fluttery' legs. Not only does this action have absolutely no effect at the time but, more to the point, the legs, those important sources of signals and information, become totally ineffective in a very short time. If the legs are used sensibly, thoughtfully, and with feel then they will transmit that emphatic signal which will be followed by a collecting and activating response.
2. Through an emphatic, impulsive action of the pelvis. This is nothing more than a momentary tilt of the pelvis.

These two actions convey to the horse the physical signal that requires the hindquarters to respond either by slowing down or speeding up. If we want to give up the indiscriminate use of the reins, then how do we communicate to the horse the small but important difference between the two?

The differentiation of the aids

There are three things we employ to clarify the difference:

1. the differentiated leg aids;

2. pelvic movement;
3. the weight aids.

1. The differentiated leg aids

The legs can be used with very subtle differences which each have very different meanings for the horse. There are four aids which are the most important.

The continuous leg aid

We have already discussed this aid and it is surely the most used and the most simple. The legs lie gently against the horse without changing their position, and remain unchanged for the duration of the riding session. For riding turns and circles, the outer leg softly increases its pressure while the inner one, barely noticeably to the horse, remains unchanged. In the first few practice sessions this inner leg should be taken a few centimetres off the horse in order to make the given aids clearer.

continuous

turns

The short, emphatic leg aid

This leg aid can be used on one side or both. One or both legs are briefly closed once to activate the haunches and collect them. This leg automatically says 'forward' to the horse. In conjunction with an appropriate weight aid and a differentiated pelvic movement, the horse can be emphatically ridden forward to a greater or lesser degree.

short emphatic

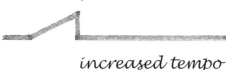

increased tempo

The short soft leg aid

This leg aid is also relatively brief and it too serves to activate the haunches and flex the hocks but it is employed comparatively softly and has a soft effect. In combination with other aids this one will signal the horse to shorten his stride or stop.

short, soft, decreasing

halts

The emphatic-intermittent leg aid

This leg aid is similar to the first one but it is applied by giving several aids in succession. It is a barely sensed, soft 'fluttering' of the knees or calf. This aid is used for the lateral movements and the High School exercises and in the most varied ways.

impulsive, emphatic-intermittent

lateral movements

Which leg aid we use depends on what we want to do. To move a horse forward, a short, emphatic leg aid serves us. To signal him to shorten his stride, we decide on the short soft aid.

2. Pelvic movement

Everything I have been saying probably sounds very complicated and, in fact, it does demand from the rider that very fine 'feel' which we usually only expect from the horses. Fundamentally, though, all of these instructions are based on the natural mechanics of movement of people as well as horses. These things do not really need to be learned, they just need to be recalled and become part of our natural existence again.

The 'pelvic dynamic' as I call it is very important and, with a highly trained horse, this signal is actually the most important. In conjunction with the precise shifting of the rider's weight, the horse is ridden and controlled exclusively through minimal changes in the position and movement of the pelvis.

In the end it is the rider's seat, his pelvis, which is in most direct contact with the horse and it is, therefore, only logical that it is here that the most important information is transmitted from one being to the other. For this reason alone, all the so-called light styles of riding are questionable because, by taking the seat out of contact with the horse, the most important and most influential method of transmitting information is sacrificed.

In order to be able to separate these pelvic movements a rider requires that close, intimate contact with the horse; the passive, quiet, following seat.

To transmit a collecting, driving aid with the pelvis, it is tilted, pushed forward, and rounded. The photographs on page 165, make this clearer. The question is, what happens just before this and what happens afterward?

I would like to explain this using the following example. The horse is moving in a nice, collected trot, the reins are looped softly, and I would like to lengthen the trot, make it more powerful for a few strides, then bring the horse back to a collected trot and then into walk.

For now we will completely ignore the varied leg and weight aids but will focus exclusively on the pelvic aid, without any help from the reins, as always.

Your upper body is very slightly behind the vertical, your legs are softly draped around the horse's belly. You allow yourself to be carried and your pelvis is **passive**, following the movement offered by the horse. Your entire body is supple and relaxed, **the legs as well as the upper body are absolutely still**. Your pelvis functions as a buffer and concussion absorber, as a moving connecting joint between you and your horse. It swings in rhythm with the horse from right to left and with every change from one side to the other it moves slightly forward. So, it is making a passive, swinging (alternating) half-circular movement.

To make the change from the collected trot into the strengthened, longer, more ground-covering trot, the pelvis must work as follows. From the passive following seat we give the horse a slightly activating forward signal through the barely perceptible forward and upward tilt of the pelvis. The horse will perceive this interruption in the smooth flow of movement at the same time as the pelvic signal gives the haunches an active push forward. The signal should be just strong, or weak, enough that the desired response results. Once it has given this active, subtle signal, the pelvis continues **actively influencing the movement of the horse** for as long as it takes the horse to adapt his motion to the 'instructions' given by the pelvic movement. Once the horse has done this, and with a trained horse it takes just fractions of a second, the pelvis goes back to its **passive following role**.

The horse will increasingly recognize as aids the 'interruptions' we consciously send him through our pelvis and he will adapt his movement accordingly. A finer means of regulating gait is barely imaginable.

Now we take the horse back to the collected trot. Again, we ignore the leg and weight aids and, as before, from the passive pelvic movement we give an active, emphatic signal, exactly as has been described above. The first emphatic, impulsive signal encourages the horse to step under and flex his hocks; that is important both for lengthening and shortening the stride. At this point, my horse does not yet know which I want.

Again the pelvis assumes an active role for as long as it takes the horse to adapt his movement to its instructions. This time, however, the pelvic rhythm is distinctly slower than that of the horse. Once the horse has shortened his stride and adapted his rhythm to that of my pelvis, then my pelvis again takes up its passive role.

All this takes only fractions of a second and after some practice it becomes automatic, a reflex.

Because of the ground work we have done, our horse is already so sensitized that it will be relatively easy to work him this way.

To go from trot to walk we proceed in the same way. Again we give the active, emphatic signal with our hips, followed immediately by pelvic movement in the rhythm of the gait we would like the horse to take, in this case the walk. You will not believe how quickly horses learn this and how very willing they are to obey our most subtle signals. But, the reward of the passive following seat must follow immediately because only then can the horse move freely under us, find a common balance with us and wholly apply himself to his work undisturbed.

In the pelvic signal for a halt, the pelvis almost mechanically comes to a halt and ceases all movement. Is that not exactly what most riders do **constantly**, no matter what the gait?

3. The weight aids

We have already spoken about weight

aids in connection with changes of direction – shifting the weight parallel to the position of the rotation of the upper body – but, in contrast, the weight aids I am discussing here are those to which, generally, no attention is paid, namely the conscious shifting of the upper body slightly forward or backward. With the various leg aids and changes in the pelvic movement, these weight aids play a very significant role in collection as well as determining tempo and rhythm.

The at-rest and working position of the rider's upper body is naturally very slightly behind the vertical. The pelvis is slightly tilted, the spine very lightly rounded. If the position of the upper body is **consciously** shifted either forward or backward (we are speaking of a few centimetres here, not shifting from a deep seat to a forward seat), it will have an effect on the horse's balance and will provoke the corresponding response.

These responses can be seen particularly well in green unspoiled horses. If they have been accustomed to the weight of the rider through preparatory exercises and their bodies have been appropriately developed and strengthened, then they will step forward if the rider's body is moved slightly backward. They are 'pushed forward' by this action and will respond in exactly the opposite way (by slowing down or halting) if the rider moves his body slightly in front of the vertical. If the upper body is taken a bit further forward an appropriately prepared horse will **step backward with no help from the reins**.

Most of the riding styles with which we are familiar make absolutely no use whatsoever of this incomparably important aid. This weight aid, like all the other subtle body signals, is given in an emphatic way and is practically invisible to an observer. Once the desired response has been obtained then, as with all the other aids, the rider slowly resumes the original position.

All three types of aids together, legs, pelvis and weight, give the horse an enormous amount of information, and, when

In general we place far too little value on the weight aids. The slight backward and forward movement of the upper body is one of the most important signals of all for the horse. A horse that is conscientiously worked using these subtle signals (together with the other aids), will eventually not only be able to be collected by a very slight forward shift of the upper body but will also move backward like clockwork, with no trouble, if the rider's upper body shifts forward a bit more. And why should he not when there are no reins for the horse to pull against, and walking backward is no problem for a fully-grown horse if he is only allowed to do it.

they are used correctly and in proper synchronization make all coarse and mechanical aids totally superfluous. With these differentiated aids and in conjunction with the preparatory exercises, every horse can be sensitized to riding by subtle means.

These aids, along with the aids for changes of direction, make up the foundation of horse-oriented collected riding with subtle body language. **That is all there is to it.** Everything that follows, all the exercises up to the highest level, build upon this base.

So, once again: **riding is very simple!** Here, once again, in overview, are the aids for regulating gait.

The young stallion Junque learns the full halt, from walk and trot, without saddle or bridle (right). Because the horse should learn to respond instantly to even the subtlest aids, as here in the halt from trot he is already stepping well under with the haunches, I always begin the exercises first without a saddle so the horse can feel the pelvic aids more easily. When those have been learned, then the exercise is repeated with a saddle.

Gait		
	Increase	Decrease	
	Emphatic tilting of the pelvis:		
	↓	↓	
1	Emphatic – short leg aid	Emphatic, slowly increasing and decreasing leg aid	1
2	Pelvic motion more active anticipating the desired rhythm	Pelvic motion less active anticipating the desired rhythm	2
3	Slight backward shift of the upper body, emphatic forward push of the horse	Minimal shift forward of the upper body	3
Once the desired response has been achieved, return to the basic position.		

All these aids can be employed so that, as they are developed, they can be almost telepathic. They are aids, minimal signals, which actually help the horse maintain his balance in every circumstance.

Here, by using the soft increasing leg aid, one emphatic tilt of the pelvis, and a barely perceptible forward shift of my upper body, I am asking the stallion to come to a collected halt from trot. Those aids are enough to help, to 'aid', this young fiery horse, who is in the early stages of his schooling, come to an anatomically correct halt. That is all there is to it! No spectacle, no show, just simple horse-oriented riding.

If there is hardly anything to be seen when giving the aids for a full halt (top) then it is impossible to photograph a half-halt. Compare the two photos above. In the one on the right you will see my legs closely hugging the horse, my back is exaggeratedly rounded and the upper body is slightly shifted forward (also exaggerated). Because I gave the aids very softly and less emphatically than for a halt, the stallion interpreted them correctly: he shortened his gait slightly, collected himself, and continued in a nicer frame.

Admittedly, what Heide is doing in the photos below

looks rather silly but, nevertheless, it helps her succeed in bringing her fireball, whom we met in the chapter on leading, to a walk from the trot on only the second day of the course. For this achievement Heide earned the spontaneous applause of the other participants, because this

little Andalusian gelding previously could be slowed down or stopped only by dropping a ship's anchor. The important thing, though, and we can see this in all the photos on this page, is that the horse stays in balance during the aid, during the halt, and then continues working still in balance.

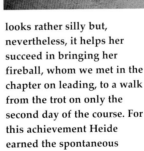

5. Collection

After we have established how we can give our horse signals for changes of gait or tempo without the mechanical use of the reins, there remains the fifth and last basic principle of riding: collection. This is not a point, however, that stands alone because all the things we have spoken about so far also serve to collect the horse, to gymnasticize him, to get him to flex the hocks, especially the aids we have just mentioned – the various leg aids, the differentiated use of the pelvis, and the use of the upper body. All have **collecting effects** and are therefore used together in a greatly reduced, barely perceptible form. After practice this will become second nature to the rider and he will then be able to use the subtle signaling potential of his body to permanently regulate the horse's collection.

From that point on, riding itself, every type of riding, whether in a dressage arena or cross-country, will serve to further collect the horse, because every piece of information transmitted to the horse has a 'collecting' character.

Nevertheless, there are a great number of meaningful exercises which serve collection in particular, the most important of which, shoulder-in, we have already spoken about in the previous chapter. (In the coming pages we will mention some important points about ridden shoulder-in.) But, all the exercises evolve very naturally from the previously mentioned riding points.

At this point, I must discuss a very important practice which, without exception, serves to both drive and collect, that is the natural use of the leg on alternate sides, evolving from the correct use of the body. I am particularly concerned that I am not misunderstood on this point. **Constant driving in rhythm with the horse's movement is to be avoided at all costs.**

When, loose and without tension, we passively follow the movement of the horse and softly drop the pelvis on one side, then the other, then the corresponding leg rests barely more strongly on the horse's side in the very split second when the hind leg on that same side is stepping forward. These minute amounts of leg pressure in that split second are enough to activate the haunches and flex the hocks.

The most important exercise for collection is riding itself. Subtle leg, pelvic, and weight aids are constant and actually help the horse to carry himself in collection. In electronics technology they speak of 'rule circles'. A system is so connected that every small irregularity is immediately corrected through the system itself. A similar system is created by rider and horse; every irregularity in the gait is responded to instantly.

Riding at last!

Starting in the basic position, shift your weight to the right and then to the left without changing the position of your spine. It is almost a parallel displacement of the entire upper body, the spine stays vertical, the shoulders remain horizontal at the same level. Practise intensively in front of a mirror. The ability to keep the spine straight and the shoulders level is the most important prerequisite to good riding! If you can do this then slowly and gradually begin a turn, a rotation of your upper body, without altering the vertical position of your spine and the horizontal position of your shoulders.

Do this slowly and thoughtfully and ask a friend to check your position for you. From this turn, go back to the position shown in the first photo. Now check once again the position of your shoulders and spine, before you return to the basic position.

When you have mastered this, go directly from the basic position into the turn as shown in photos three to six, shifting your body weight in the desired direction at the same time while keeping your hips and shoulders parallel. Once again, you cannot overestimate the value of this exercise: it is the foundation of all good riding.

Finally! The time has come to carry everything we have learned over to riding. We have prepared ourselves appropriately, have suppled and sensitized our body so that there is a good chance we will not be an undue burden to our horse and, most importantly, not a harmful one.

During many practice sessions and many hours spent with our horse we have won his complete trust. We are totally respected by him and accepted as his herd leader. Our horse has become so strengthened and suppled that he is able to carry us with ease. Through all of our exercises he carries himself in a shortened, collected frame, working more and more on the haunches which we have activated and strengthened.

Nevertheless, we will approach the first ridden exercises slowly and step by step so that the skill and dexterity of our horses can gradually grow along with our increasing confidence.

So, we begin our work by allowing ourselves to be led on straight tracks so that we can, without distractions, feel everything we have previously practised on the ground. The actual work then begins in the picadero, where, in an environment which the horse already trusts, we will try to really find our way into, and follow, the horse's movement. Our goal is to do just this, undisturbed by any reining or 'steering' work. We can carefully attempt the first full and half-halts and take pleasure in how precisely and promptly our horse responds.

In the picadero work, we develop a good soft seat which follows the horse's movement. The halts and half-halts succeed promptly so that with voltes, turns, and larger circles we prepare our horse, and ourselves too, for riding in the countryside, through fields and forest. The reins always hang loosely, and we find ourselves in a mutual balance with our partner which is never disturbed by the gross use of the reins.

Now exercises can be added which supple the horse more, making him handier and more rideable, more self-confident and collected: the small circles and figures-of-eight, the turns on the haunches and, finally, the shoulder-in.

The lunge work has long been moved outside the picadero and varied and broadened with a large number of exercises.

We have made good progress on our journey to the stars. The work with our horse is now always very quiet and peaceful. We have been able to set aside all negative feelings – the annoyance, the anger, the ambition – when we are together with our friend. We have become a quiet, patient observer and always think, see, hear, and feel more and more in the consciousness of our horse, who now yields to us patiently and reliably. We have become a horsewoman, a horseman.

We have not trained our horse, we have educated him. We have not forced him, rather we have patiently and lovingly established trust and physical, as well as psychological, security.

But, we have not really reached quite that far yet. So, let us ask someone to help us with the first exercises on the horse. In my courses I treat all participants the same, regardless of their experience with horses; all are 'beginners', everyone starts all over again. No matter how many trophies you have won, please consider whether it might not nevertheless make sense for you to do all these exercises in sequence.

Exercises without a saddle

The first exercises should be done without a saddle if possible. This will help you establish a good seat and, above all, to discover the horse's rhythm of movement. If you cannot vault lightly onto your horse then ask someone to give you a leg up. What is important is that you settle **very softly** on to your horse's back. This should happen in slow motion so that you do not cause unnecessary stress to the most sensitive part of his body.

Please study the photographs on pages 173–181. They illustrate exactly what we are trying to accomplish.

The correct seat

The very first thing we should do is try to find a comfortable, natural sitting position. Since you are sitting on the horse without a saddle this should be fairly simple. Your upper body will be very slightly behind the vertical. Do not be ashamed to let yourself be led like a beginner, because that way, sometimes even with your eyes closed, is the best way to feel the rhythm of your horse's movement. Place your hand on your navel and make sure that the movement of the horse does not carry over to the upper body.

In addition, make certain that you are sitting absolutely straight on your horse, that your weight is distributed equally between the two halves of your seat and that your shoulders are always carried level.

Ask a friend to check your position, or, even better, have your position videoed.

Most riders, who do not consciously work at this, sit crookedly on their horses, which leads to an uneven burdening of one side and therefore to undesired movements from the horse. These 'disobediences' are then followed by the 'corrective' jab of the spurs, from which the only thing the horse learns is: do not react to shifts in weight because, if you do, punishment follows.

Feeling the hind leg

Now, close your eyes and try to feel when the right and then the left hind leg is starting its stride. As we have already mentioned, when the hind leg lifts the croup sinks down, which is transmitted to the back.

The person leading your horse or another observer will confirm the correctness of your observations.

Here is a snapshot which shows a confident pair from behind. You can see how really straight, how vertical, Insa sits on her horse, with the shoulders level. This is not always the case: most riders place an uneven burden on their horses.

The first ridden exercises in the picadero

The first riding lessons inside the picadero should be done with a partner who can, from the ground, support the rider's aids. At the beginning, the halt exercises will look a little funny. Nevertheless, the horse responds absolutely correctly and stands square. From the beginning, the horse halts on the haunches. The rider's aids are continually refined until the horse responds as though guided by a spirit hand.

At first we want to concentrate on two things: a truly good seat, that intimate connection with the horse's back, and learning the full and half-halts. That means **you** need to learn these things since our horse, by nature, already has the ability to respond appropriately to the correct signals.

When I school young horses or correct

horses that have already had some schooling – the latter being much harder than the former – then, as a rule, I proceed in exactly the same sequence. The system that I am passing on to you with all these exercises was not intended merely for learning to ride. It is meant for everyday work. Anything which has proven to be good and right for the one purpose cannot be totally wrong for the other.

Just as I always do, you should begin with a trusted assistant. This person should be so familiar with the principles of the lunge and picadero work that, at least for the time being, he can take your place on the ground.

The progression is very simple. For the horse, hardly anything changes; as before he does his turns and performs his exercises, only now he is doing this with you on his back. Your assistant, in the middle of the arena, will be 'central command' for your horse in the following lessons and all you have to do is concentrate on always finding your way gently into the movement and following it! You make sure that your upper body is still and that your legs hang loosely and gently against your horse's belly. You repeatedly feel and identify which hind leg is lifting and ask the person on the ground to correct you when necessary.

Now you begin work on the halt. It is simplest for you and your horse if you start by going from trot to walk. That nearly always works, and your horse will grasp very quickly what it is you want.

Tip your pelvis forward in an emphatic way, allow the upper body to lean **very slightly** forward and **gently**, for a brief moment, close your legs.

In the early stages, when these aids are still uncoordinated and exaggerated, it looks to

an observer as though the rider is collapsing due to a severe stomach cramp. It does not matter if it does look like that, it means that you are proceeding correctly. The main thing is that your horse understands you, and I am sure he will. The niceties and subtleties will come with time and then the observer will see nothing (and develop stomach cramps himself out of sheer envy!).

For the first two or three attempts your assistant in the middle will support your signals with his own body language but, after a while, that help can be done without. **Do not forget to praise, and only practise for a few moments.** It is better to stop work frequently and begin anew after an appropriate pause. Allow plenty of time for everything, and do not practise the same thing several days in a row. That would become too boring for you and for your horse.

Next you can halt from the walk, then halt from the trot and, when your horse is ready, you can ask for a halt from the canter.

You can sit and halt or half-halt your horse in collection without rein aids; only turning remains.

For the first turning exercises we will use a helpful tool that I use to make my work easier. All the arenas I had worked in, even a picadero, seemed too large a space in which to teach a horse, who is unused to being ridden in this way, to turn in the way we want. My students and my horses needed to learn the use of the leg and weight aids in the simplest way possible, and so the surveyor's-tape lane was born. This has proved to be an indispensable tool for me when developing a horse.

Here we encounter the basic principle of structuring and presenting the exercises to horse and rider in such a way that conflicts are avoided.

I often have a helper for my work in the picadero. Here Alberto is helping me by taking a particular position in the picadero and by vibrating the lunge at very specific moments so that my horse becomes sensitized to my specific aids.

The surveyor's-tape lane

Gisela on her mare in the surveyor's-tape lane. Because of the tight boundaries, the possibilities for changes of direction are very limited, so it is possible to work right from the start with the most subtle aids. Gisela sits straight and without tension on her horse, the horse has no problem following the correct signals, positions herself and moves in the desired direction.

In a riding arena, or better yet out in the open with several trees for help, set the boundaries for your riding lane with the surveyor's tape. This is available in hardware, building supply, or do-it-yourself shops. To begin with, your lane should be fairly narrow, around 4 or 5 m (13 ft–16 ft 6 in wide). The length does not matter too much but the minimum length should be 15–20 m (49 ft 3 in–65 ft 6 in).

Gisela on her mare in the surveyor's-tape lane. Because of the tight boundaries, the possibilities for changes of direction are very limited, so it is possible to work right from the start with the most subtle aids. Gisela sits straight and without tension on her horse, the horse has no problem following the correct signals, positions herself and moves in the desired direction.

Often it is helpful to reinforce the body signals with some sort of tool (in this case the whip) in order to make them clearer and more precise. Gabi is holding the whip horizontally in order to make the turn signal clearer to her horse.

We are not going to do much with this lane to start with; the horse is really limited to going straight ahead, and that is exactly what he should be doing. We will tack him up with a simple halter and one or two lead ropes and walk him straight ahead. At the end of the lane he will have

Often it is helpful to reinforce the body signals with some sort of tool (in this case the whip) in order to make them clearer and more precise. Gabi is holding the whip horizontally in order to make the turn signal clearer to her horse.

to turn right or left and it is here that we come into action. We apply the outside leg (i.e. the opposite leg to the direction of the turn) and shift our weight to the inside as we rotate the shoulders and the upper body in the direction of the turn, while we remain sitting straight (spine vertical, shoulders level, no collapsing of the hip or the waist), and, already our horse is turning **without rein aids** in the direction we have asked him to go. In a very short time this will be working so well that, within our lane we will be able to ride figures-of-eight, voltes and serpentines, always with the lead lines/reins hanging loosely.

Your assistant will tell you, a video will show you but, above all, your horse and your own 'feel' will let you know whether or not you are sitting correctly. It is a wonderful feeling to have truly helped your horse through the turn and is 'help' not the very meaning of aid? Your horse will not need the four or five metres; he will turn like an eel and, supported by his deeply stepping-under hindquarters he will hug the turn totally stable and in perfect tempo.

Now you can take all the exercises out of the picadero into the tape lane, and vary the work as much as possible. It is nice when there are trees in the middle of the lane that you can weave around. In this way the horse comes to realize just why all the voltes and circles are being ridden.

Finally, you can make the lane into an L-shape to provide a corner and gradually widen it. You can put poles down and trot over or between them, or canter and jump them. You can build bridges or see-saws, or borrow an entire trail course from the Western riders but just be sure that you do everything in balance with your horse and always with loosely hanging reins! Be creative and original, your horse will become

enthralled with the work and will love playing around and experimenting.

At this point all that remains is for me to tell you about the soft aids for the walk, trot, and canter departs. A slight backward movement of your upper body, a barely perceptible push of your hips, and to 'think' about the desired gait rhythm are enough. If your horse has responded soft-ly and fluidly in the appropriate way,

Far left Trixi's Arabian gelding responds promptly to the signal of a cocked pelvis and a slight shift in weight. Trixi is not even using the leg aids, since the horse would, at this point, still interpret them as driving aids. It will take time for him to correctly interpret the different leg aids in conjunction with the other aids.

Left Bettina is in the surveyor's-tape lane for the first time. She is totally unaccustomed to turning and halting her horse without any rein influence but her confidence grows as she experiences her horse responding consistently to these simple aids. In the first photo we see that Bettina is nicely turned in the direction of movement, but that her inside leg is still on the horse and she has not shifted her weight to the right seat bone quite correctly. It is important to always allow someone to watch you and check your position. The aid to halt is very precise, and the horse responds promptly.

Right The exercises give little Judith a great deal of pleasure. In the second photo we can see how, at the beginning, her inner leg is clearly stretched away from the horse. That is totally correct at this point, to better distinguish the aid. After some practice sessions though, the leg aid should be invisibly given through a slight lessening or increasing of pressure. Judith had some problems with the correct rotation of her upper body but in the third picture it is better.

Below right **Ingrid on her pinto. In the top photo we see that the right shoulder is significantly lower than the left but in the two lower photos, from a corrected position, the rotation and weight displacement are very nice.**

return to the normal position immediately, a hair behind the vertical, allow a little pelvic and leg action (we are talking about movements that are barely perceptible) in order to scoop your horse upward into the next gait, establish him in the tempo you require and to collect and stabilize him there.

Basically, your body is perpetually in barely perceptible motion in order to maintain the desired tempo, the pure rhythm, and optimum collection. After a number of exercises and a lot of practice this will happen automatically, just like walking and running, which you had to learn with a great deal of effort as a small child. In the end, the horse's four legs become ours. They respond purely to thought, to every subconscious signal. We have melted into one with our horse!

Advanced work in the picadero

After all of that, we find ourselves in the picadero once again in order to further educate our horse and ourselves. Naturally, the ground work and the work on the lunge line continue to be further refined and perfected; they remain part of our work for as long as we work with horses.

We cannot do without the picadero, no matter how well we think the riding is coming along!

The picadero can be adapted to many riding exercises. Because of its proportions and relatively small size, all sorts of beautiful and useful figures can be ridden which continually develop the handiness and rideability of our horses. The drawings on page 179 suggest several possibilities. These can be endlessly varied and ridden in all gaits. In the meantime we will work with a good saddle and one day we will start working with four loose reins. More about this in the following sections.

The last picadero exercise illustrated on page 179, the riding of diagonal voltes, should be a big part of your exercise programme in this phase of schooling and should be done surely, precisely and exclusively through subtle body signals because it is this exercise which will lead us into the most important one, the ridden shoulder-in.

When the time has come to refine the basic exercises through variations in the picadero work and we have employed the appropriate bit and bridle for that, we should always be sure that we continue to ride our horse with our body, not with the mechanical employment of the reins. Every rider should be able to ride his horse bridleless, in every gait, just as Margaret demonstrates here with her Camargue mare. Naturally, you should take all safety precautions and establish good boundaries.

The range of exercise variations is nearly limitless. The pole work demonstrated here is not only good schooling for the horse, it is also good for developing the rider's seat, since, in trotting over the poles, the horse's back really swings. Because the horse goes into the exercise completely freely it is, as a rule, not a problem to complete since the horse can find his own rhythm and tempo, without any hindering reins.

Six exercise patterns but the possible variations are countless, use your imagination.

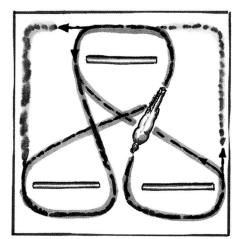
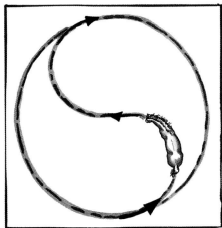
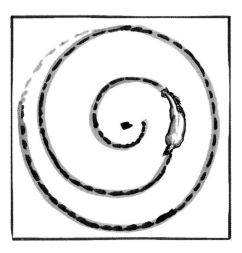
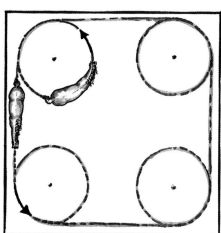
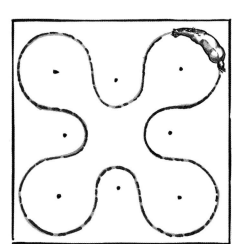
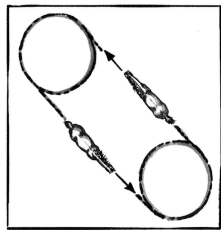

Little Janosch is observing my activities with great interest. Very quickly the poles are laid in the shape of an 'L'. In the course of this work the horses become unbelievably aware and they learn to see the world through human eyes! This small horse in particular continually surprises me with his awareness and intelligence. When uninitiated observers watch us at work, they often do not quite trust their impressions. They feel as though they are in a movie in which the abilities of the horse are portrayed as a caricature of those of human beings.

But, nevertheless, it is true that horses visibly open themselves to further communication the instant they find an understandable quality in the countenance of human beings. They 'engage' themselves in the dialogue and actively learn to better comprehend and understand people.

As can readily be seen by Janosch's reaction in the first three pictures, the world of humans is no longer something totally abstract to which a horse pays no attention. It is now something that has meaning for him, something worth observing.

When a horse is steered through such lanes and alleys it has a very positive effect in that the horse learns to very precisely associate the different aids with the specific exercises. The learning achievement is therefore quite great.

After the horse was halted with a short signal, he was asked to step backward out of the 'L'; even with reins this is not a simple exercise but without them the horse must respond to very fine weight aids. Carefully, and step by step, the horse is ridden through the narrow turn. The signal for backing up is a slight tilting forward of the upper body and the alternating light leg aids which support the horse in the backward movement.

Because the horse was worked precisely with the weight aids up to this point, he responds promptly to the forward tip of the rider's upper body with backward steps.

A slight taking back of the upper body and an even slighter pelvic aid allow the horse to slow down and step backward in a tempo determined by the rider.

The speed can be regulated extremely finely and precisely with the slight backward and forward movement of the rider's upper body as a weight aid. Exercises of this type have the additional benefit of increasing the horse's self-awareness. In a very subtle way he begins taking himself and his body seriously. Therefore none of these exercises are done just for their own sake. Their effect extends well beyond the obvious physical benefits.

The shoulder-in under saddle

With the instructions for this, probably the most important exercise of all, we approach the conclusion of this book. Everything that has gone before, as well as this exercise, belongs in the repertoire of every riding session. Everything beyond this builds on this foundation and develops practically on its own, if you have worked patiently and in a horse-oriented way.

This exercise, correctly ridden, will, like no other, unite horse and rider in a common balance, and will show the horse how he can best carry the combined weight. From here to piaffe is just a small step.

The first thing, which we must always keep in mind is that **practically no aids are needed in the performance of this exercise**. Were I to approach the work as it is commonly done with gross and complicated aids, I might succeed in bending my horse a little but this would have nothing to do with a stable, solidly ridden shoulder-in. No horse can be gymnasticized and developed in that way.

First of all, be clear about all the things you should *not* do before you begin this exercise: you work with virtually no additional aids and never pull on the inside rein!

Let us take the exercise step by step.

We want to develop the shoulder-in from the last picadero exercise, the diagonal voltes. But this time the horse does not leave the voltes positioned straight on the diagonal line but, instead, on a distinct angle to it. The volte is already well known and understood by our horse. After three voltes he will anticipate the change through the arena. We will use this to our advantage (again, as a little plaster cast for the nerves!) and, we will use everything that has been taught in this book. The horse must position himself because of the rotation of the rider's body and allow himself to be ridden on the circle. He must be familiar with and accept

the weight displacement, both forward and back, of the rider's upper body as an aid. He must also instantly respond to the laid-on leg and to a sideways weight displacement by stepping under and following it. In other words, he must display all the sensitivity that can be achieved through our way of working.

The illustration below will clarify the progression of this exercise.

We start by riding the change through the arena a few times. It is important that

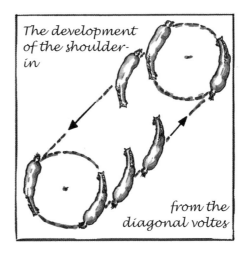

The development of the shoulder-in from the diagonal voltes

we always ride the same number of voltes so that our horse anticipates the change. As we achieve the angle of the shoulder-in, the horse will want to move to the opposite corner of the arena, thus supporting our intention. After we have ridden, for example, the third volte cleanly, instead of straightening the horse coming out of the turn, we continue two or three steps more on the arc of the circle, therefore putting more weight on the inside seat bone, maintaining the inward rotation of the upper body and letting the outside leg lie unchanged. In the moment where we achieve the correct angle/position for the shoulder-in we do four things,

After the young stallion has been worked on the lunge line and in the picadero, once the weight aids for riding turns and voltes have been made clear to him and after he has learned to completely accept full halts and has begun to understand the idea of half-halts, his schooling in bending, flexion and collection can be advanced with the exercise of shoulder-in. The photos on this and the next page were made during a schooling session and clarify the interplay of ground work and work under saddle. The work on the diagonal is understood so well by the stallion because of the prior work in-hand that, now, without saddle or bitted bridle, with the very subtlest aids, a balanced, unhindered shoulder-in is rideable without further practice. The horse is already positioned, although the horizontal flexion will be further perfected during the coming weeks and months. Note that the rider's shoulders are level. The horse is not, as is so commonly done, being pushed into this exercise. Meaningful weight aids enable him to perform the exercise independently, expressively, and undisturbed.

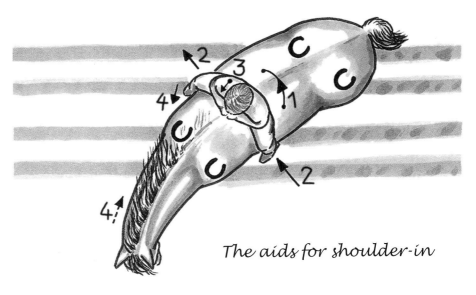

The aids for shoulder-in

preferably simultaneously.
On a volte left.

1. **With the inward rotation of the upper body unchanged** we displace our weight to the right, thereby burdening the horse on the outside. Because of the position of the upper body and the horse's direction of movement this is not easy but, it means that we **do not**, as is so often seen, collapse to the inside and virtually push the horse into the exercise. In collapsing to the inside we burden the inner side of the horse, who then is barely able to step forward and under powerfully and undisturbed. But, when we put our weight to the outside, we leave the inside free so that our horse can step under the body weight unhindered and expressively. It is very important that the rider's **shoulders always remain level**.

2. At the same time we change the leg pressure. The outer leg is taken off the horse a minimal amount and the inner leg is laid on. Through the continuously maintained rotation of the rider's upper body, the horse's position will stay unchanged. Because of the weight shifting right and because of the laid-on left leg, the horse will automatically travel on the diagonal at the desired angle. So that the horse does not escape forward, it is necessary that we . . .

3. . . . very slightly, and barely perceptibly move the upper body forward a bit while applying both legs for a fraction of a second, i.e. give a half-halt. The upper body's forward movement is barely perceptible but the horse responds promptly because of all the previous practice.) This is all a question of feel because now a number of things happen at once. In order to really maintain the chosen angle/position a fourth thing may be necessary.

4. The right leg, which has been taken slightly off the horse's side moves a hair's

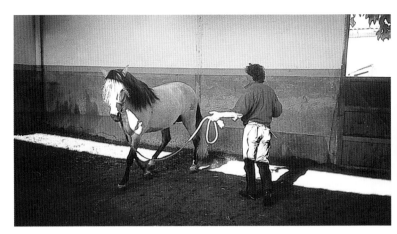

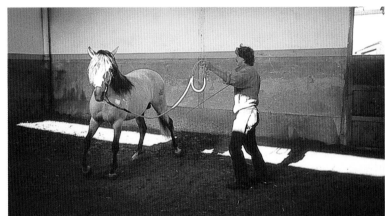

Here we see once more three phases of the preparatory work in-hand. In the early stages of ridden shoulder-in, the horse should always be asked first for one or two reprises in-hand, so that he recognizes what the trainer is working on. The horse comes out of the volte on the loosely hanging lunge line. In the moment that the position for shoulder-in is achieved, the horseman carefully raises the leading hand in order to half-halt the horse; the leading hand, whip and body movement combine to enable the horse to do the exercise without any mechanical influence or stress. Bend and position will be perfected in the course of time.

Out of the precisely ridden shoulder-in the piaffe can later be developed. The rider can completely forsake the usually employed restraining rein aids: the equilibrium is perfect.

breadth forward, and thus nearer the forehand. In the moment that the left hind leg steps forward we apply the right leg for a tiny moment and support this signal with a light vibration of the **loosely hanging** right rein. This is enough to keep the horse in his position. The inside (left) leg aid then follows intermittently in the course of the exercise. That means the leg pressure is not constant, but is always increased by a minute amount when the left hind leg steps forward, thus the inside (left) hind leg is given an emphatic stimulus which allows it to step deeply and powerfully under the body.

Let us clarify all this once more.

The angle of the horse is established, maintained or corrected by the appropriate rotation of the rider's upper body. Supporting this, at the beginning, is the non-driving leg in connection with a

simultaneous short rein signal (but always with loosely hanging reins).

Under no circumstances do we employ the inside rein. This would immediately throw the horse on the forehand and ruin the work.

All this will work but everything requires time. To begin with we must be satisfied with small successes. After two steps of shoulder-in on the diagonal we straighten the horse and give him plenty of praise. The best thing is to dismount immediately and lead him to his stall or paddock, that way a good impression of the work remains fresh in his mind. Soon, always supported by shoulder-in in-hand, the horse will do the entire diagonal line in a clean shoulder-in.

Once we have achieved that we can begin to practise this exercise anywhere in the picadero.

Advanced Leading and Lunge Work

It is great that you have followed me to this point. All that remains is for me to show you the interplay of the most important elements and expand upon them. The demands we make on ourselves are now as high as the goal that previously seemed unreachable. We want to dominate without punishing, but truly dominate. Collect without reins, but truly collect. Act without intended goals, but truly act.

By understanding the work, the horse's willingness to participate and to please the horseman will eventually become so great that the horse, at liberty, can be directed over jumps he could easily avoid. The lunge line, loosely draped around the horse's neck, no longer offers any real means to direct him, to turn him or to stop him. It is now a subtle, symbolic connection to the horseman. The horse acts and reacts of his own free will.

Anti-authoritarian upbringing?

A learning method can only be as good or as bad as it is rightly or wrongly understood and I want to be certain that you understand me correctly! You have worked your way through this book and by doing so have gained a very thorough, complex understanding of the fundamental principles of this way of teaching and working. But, before I instruct you how to go even further, I would like to go over the most important points once more.

The fundamental idea of this working method is that we are not training and suppressing, but giving the horse every possible freedom. That is possible only when there is mutual awareness and respect; I must respect the horse but it is essential that the horse also respects me.

The method, which I have attempted to present as completely as possible in this book brings with it a danger, i.e. an anti-authoritarian upbringing.

Anti-authoritarian upbringing does not mean that every sort of regulation, every type of framework, all structure is given up. On the contrary, anti-authoritarian upbringing is less about the result than about the means employed to achieve it. The practitioner must, on principle, abstain from authoritarian methods of discipline but other methods must replace these if everything is not to disintegrate into anarchy and ruin. These alternate methods, however, demand a **much greater discipline**, a much greater **self-control** on the part of the 'upbringer' than the authoritarian principles of old.

'Upbringing' is probably the word chosen by the inventors of the method, otherwise it would not be called anti-authoritarian *upbringing* but rather anti-authoritarian *chaos*, which is exactly what has resulted in many cases.

Chaos could also endanger the path we follow. There must be something to replace conspicuous authority, regimentation and punishment but it must be completely clear and consistent.

In this book I have given you a clue, a direction, to this path. Now you are being asked to fill this path with your own unique personality. Every horse is unique every horseman is unique. Set recipes constrict you but guiding principles bring understanding and provide a foundation on which each person can build, using the methods at hand.

The path I wanted to show you is one that leads to a more primal, more natural, more loving and freer orientation to the horse, and to all the knowledge, understanding and insight this brings.

The play of powers

If we oppress any living creature – a child, a horse, a woman, an underling, a student, a foreigner – if we humiliate them, then we force them to retreat within themselves or to protest loudly, or silently, but in the end we will break them. The play of powers is unequal, there are predictable winners and losers.

We do not break our horses, we do the opposite, we enhance, we develop, we bring out powers where, before, barely any were perceived. The play of powers becomes ever more equal, but what does that mean for us? That we constantly ascertain that we can in fact manage those spirits we bring to fruition!

Our horse's self-confidence, power and self-assertion increases with each lesson. Our protégé will not just want to fight for a higher-ranking position within a herd of horses, he will also observe us very closely to see if we are still powerful enough to retain the role we pretend to play.

We must develop along with our horse, and we must both learn from one another. You will find the means to do this in this book, what you do with them depends entirely on you.

There is something else with regard to this that I want to make very clear. Many of the pictures in this book look like a collection of works of art. But that is definitely not meant to be the case. I refrain from any sort of showing off because it is entirely self-serving and only in the rarest of circumstances beneficial to the horse. In my eyes a horse is not a wind-up toy. When in the course of his education a horse has achieved a certain level, then it belongs to the past – even when he has mastered that step to the point of perfection.

- We interfere as little as possible in the life of the horse.
- The horse always receives the maximum freedom possible from us.
- No dressage, no 'show effects'. Rather, a slow getting-accustomed-to-one-another, a slow flowing together of the spheres of each other's lives through a gentle, dominant, horse-oriented interaction.
- No routine and no recipes but, instead, creativity, expertise, intuition, and individual personality.

Meadow, forest, stick and stone

This is the world of the horse; this is his nature. And, as often as possible, I pack my odds and ends and take off with my horse. I take a piece of surveyor's tape

with me, a lead rope, a lunge line and off we go! Riding, leading, lungeing, taking a walk, loafing, spending days on the road – out in the country there is enough space to do everything. Most importantly, it is never boring, not for us and not for the horses.

Variety, variety

This is our motto. Horses in nature are really like all free creatures, uninterruptedly busy, caught up in their need to survive, to procreate. They are exposed to endless stimulations all of which trigger a response. This is nature's way of ensuring that horses adapt to changing circumstances and evolve.

This awareness, this 'aliveness' which is continually fostered by nature is something we must bring into and retain in our work.

Boredom monotony and routine are inimical to our work and to life. We should, therefore, always be conscious of making the work as interesting and as varied as possible. I will give you some suggestions on the following pages.

Let us now begin the advanced lunge work.

Continually increasing the challenge

We have learned to understand the many-faceted signals of our horse, so we can quickly recognize when the time comes to increase the difficulty of the work, to increase the challenge.

This is an important and sensitive issue that must be kept in delicate balance. If the challenges are too easily met, boredom and lack of enthusiasm sneak in. If they are too difficult, we overface our horse physically or psychologically, thereby creating the corresponding 'resistance' and 'fight' responses. Even the first small indications of these responses will, as a rule, make rougher aids necessary. But, if we skilfully combine, slowly but steadily, more difficult assignments with an always varied and interesting work programme, then, most of the problem areas are avoided from the very beginning.

In the long run we can only expect from our horses the creativity that we ourselves are prepared to give. An uncreative human being will, in time, turn his sensitive, aware animal into a plodding nag. But, that also works in reverse, many a plodding nag becomes a spirited, fiery mount after just a short spell of creative, horse-oriented work.

Leading from the fourth position

After we have mastered the work in the picadero and the work on the lunge line, and our horse participates joyfully and with interest, we should begin to change the leading position for certain exercises. As with the work on the lunge line we position ourselves at the level of the croup, but we move closer to the horse and, in this way, walk with him where we please. We turn the horse solely by moving the leading hand to the left or to the right and take care that our horse **always accepts and respects the draping lunge line!**

With surveyor's tape or some other material, we mark out a 10 x 20 m picadero. This allows space for two 10 m circles. In order to change from one circle to the other, we send our horse straight down the long side to take him on to the second circle.

To begin with we place a jumping pole parallel to the boundary. If our horse realizes what is expected of him and lets himself be led through this little alley onto the

other circle merely by the use of hand signals, then we can begin to vary the work. We can halt the horse in the alley, ask him to go backward, ask him to trot off from the back-up, etc.

Soon the horse will accept our new position as normal even while being lead, so then we can do without the pole and work in this position **on both sides of the horse equally** outside the practice area. However, this position is always something very special. It should only be used for very particular exercises; the normal leading position is from the side, ahead of the nostrils.

Here we see Claudia with her mare, who at the beginning was not easy to deal with. However, after several weeks of meaningful work even this horse could be worked from this difficult position without problems. What is important is that the horse has learned to respect the loosely draped lead line in absolutely every situation. If the horse begins to resist, the horseman is, in this position, hopelessly subordinate to the animal.

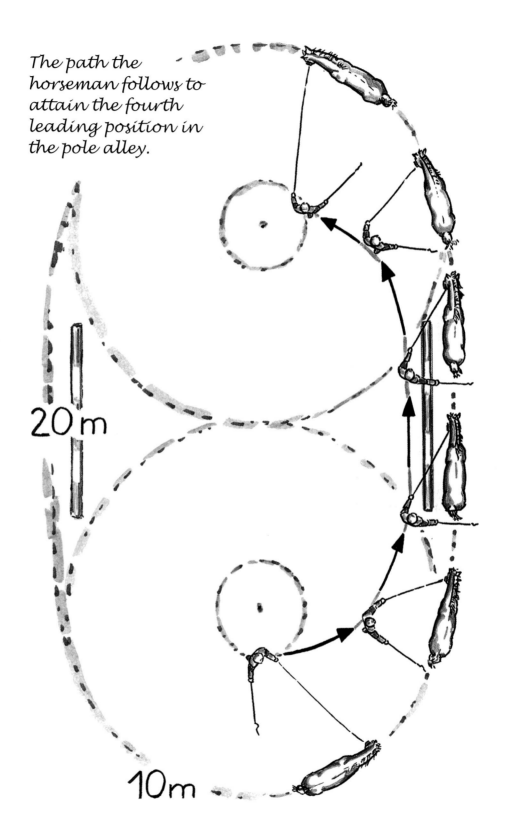

The path the horseman follows to attain the fourth leading position in the pole alley.

20 m

10 m

The horse trailer and other obstacles

From the fourth position we can now challenge our horse with all sorts of obstacles and 'difficulties'. Dominance and trust have been so consolidated that our horse deals independently with the challenges presented to him. It is important that we always approach things with a great deal of patience. We never pressure a horse. Instead we give him the opportunity to **overcome the obstacle independently and with confidence**.

Once the horse has done this he is praised generously and, on the following day, presented with the same obstacle. With the successful experience still very vivid in his memory he will now hesitate much less and **joyfully** complete his assignment. In this way, even apparently unpleasant things like loading onto a trailer become independent, joyful actions. Be creative! Believe me, your horse will become more demanding day by day, and will expect ever greater challenges from you. If, after a few weeks of such work you do not, at the very least, land a helicopter in your riding arena, you will receive a bored, pitying look from your horse! But do not at this stage make the mistake of giving your horse unclear instructions or tasks for which he is not prepared. Make continual progress, but in small steps.

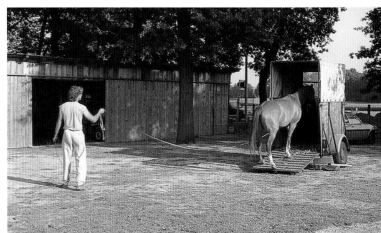

From this leading position the horse can easily meet and solve all the problems presented to him, because he is left to work it out for himself, with curiosity and courage. Trailer loading becomes an interesting puzzle which the horse solves ever more independently. As you can see, the lunge line gets longer and longer as the horse finds his own way in. It is critical that we increase the difficulty of these exercises very slowly and allow the horse time to develop his curiosity and conquer his fear.

Leading with the lasso: work in the open

Now the fruits of your work will reveal themselves almost on their own and will seem just as natural as they were once thought impossible.

Now you can hang a thin rope, a simple lasso, around your horse's neck and play around with leading in all positions since the dominance question has long since been resolved. Through all the work that has been done so far, your horse has become so accustomed to a fine connection between you that he will accept it in this form too! Leading and taking walks together becomes a free, uncomplicated game. The boundary indicated by the line is always accepted **without a struggle**! You should make certain of that before taking this step.

In the end, you can do without even this simple rope and work your horse completely at liberty in large fenced-in fields. Your horse will follow you and will want to play and work with you like a small dog, but with the total dignity, the total pride and the total self-confidence which only a horse can possess. Remember, to bring a dog so far is easy, but a horse . . . a horse requires so much more. If you are successful in this work then you will be very close to your horse, to nature, and to life itself.

Only a few weeks have passed since this little stallion became accustomed to the hand of man. In the meantime he has learned to respond to the most subtle signals. The wild horse has become a horse who not only tolerates the presence of man but actually desires it and seeks it. With only a simple lasso draped around his neck, I no longer have power over the horse if he takes it into his head to run away. With a gelding or a mare, that is one thing, with a stallion it is something quite different; walking past the mares being led in this way displays unbelievable trust and respect. Please do this only when you are completely sure of what you are doing.

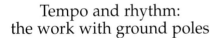

Far Left Gabi did not believe that her mare who once struck, kicked and bucked like a rodeo horse would ever respond to such fine subtle signals while at liberty. In the course of time Gabi developed her own unmistakable style of body language, and her horse responds very sensitively to it. All this is only possible when trust has reached a very high level, because the shy, cat-like part of the horse's nature must be totally won over by the horseman.

Naturally, every horse will run to his owner from the paddock once in a while. But, it is communication that makes a coincidental occurrence something that can be controlled. Even here it is not about an effect that might favourably impress an observer but more about the steadily growing togetherness of two beings who, in the end, can rely totally on one another.

Tempo and rhythm: the work with ground poles

Wherever you wish – in the picadero, in the riding arena, or somewhere in an open field – you can work with jump poles and cavalletti. Three, four or five poles laid at a distance of about 1 m apart improve the horse's trot as well as his action, his tempo and his feel for rhythm. This work is very strenuous for the horse, so only incorporate a few minutes of it in the daily work. This type of pole work will discipline us, and our horses, to work precisely. For that reason alone, you should go back to it frequently.

Logs, barrels and small jumps

We have learned to work our horse on a loose lunge line, to send him in all directions, and to have him change direction through the circle. It is a good test of obedience to see if the horse will, *exclusively* through the use of fine, subtle signals, allow himself to be directed over obstacles. In addition, it is exceptionally useful for developing the hindquarters of the horse if he jumps over **small** obstacles out of the trot. This exercise will loosen and strengthen our horse. But be careful, it is very easy to overstep the bounds of what is useful.

Left These photos, taken on the second day of one of my courses, prove that what we have discussed in this book is not *just* training. Even horses who, by nature, are not among the most sensitive, and have previously been shown the way only with the most drastic methods, suddenly, from one moment to the next, behave in a way that completely surprises their owners. Ingrid could barely believe that it was her horse who, after a short pause, came to her in the riding arena and willingly followed her without a lead line.

Once again we see little Janosch, here working over ground poles and obstacles. We can see how the horse accepts the lunge line (lasso) as our fine connection, and follows the signals of my hand and my body. Because the horse is free he can easily negotiate the obstacle, and, unencumbered, choose his own tempo and rhythm. These photos show how the horse adjusts his balance to the various tasks.

Lanes, markers and turning points

As a rule our horse can understand only with great difficulty why he must halt, turn, or move backwards at a particular spot. It becomes much more comprehensible and interesting for him if we make some sense of these actions with the use of barrels, poles, surveyor's-tape lanes, and other markers. In addition, these tools always inspire new variations in the exercises and, not least, they accustom us to working with precision because now it is not enough to make a turn just anywhere, but it should be done at a particular point.

The poles and obstacles can be used in a wide variety of ways. The horse responds ever more sensitively to the problems posed and, ever more independently, finds solutions. He learns to recognize and understand the world of humans more and more clearly. A heartfelt thank you to this boy who has been so charming a guide throughout this book!

The four most important nerve points

I tie in massaging the point between the ears with gently encouraging a lowering of the head in order to further both dominance and trust in equal measure (far right).

Good, intimate, meaningful work with the horse must encompass all conceivable areas. The horse, not infrequently finds the ways in which we handle him to be uncomfortable and intrusive. But there are four points that deserve special attention. When touching a horse on these four

Massaging the dock is an age old method for retaining the affection of a horse. Here in Spain, in the land of the *gitanos*, the gypsies, it is an old, much used method. It relaxes a horse from head to toe and makes him peaceful and attentive. It is important always to be careful and to observe the horse's reactions so that we can orient ourselves to him. As with everything, use, and trust, your intuition (right).

This photo shows the young stallion once again on the second day after our meeting. Again and again I extend my hand to the horse in order to gently play with his nostrils (below).

points, you can, as a rule, observe a relaxing effect within moments. These points are: the nostril area, the point between the ears, the withers area and the dock.

Nerve clusters are found around the nostrils and on the dock, the touching of which produces a calming and relaxing effect. This explains the effect of the apparently brutal horse twitch; the horse is not bedeviled by pain but quietened by endorphins released into the brain.

Please begin your own attempts carefully and observe your horse's response.

About punishment and release

We have spoken quite a lot about punishing versus not punishing, dominance and trust, but punishment, as such, has been purely and simply eliminated. This must always be the case, even though the time has come to bring the phenomenon of punishment under closer scrutiny.

To establish a better understanding of this I break it down into three types of action. The first is **punishment**, the second is **protection of personal space** and the third is **the use of dominance tools/aids**.

In my experience the theoretical-sounding differences between these things actually have, in practice, great significance.

Punishment

1. Punishment is tied in with emotion; annoyance, anger, rage, loss of control, lack of restraint, falling out of a role, etc. Experience proves that just the appearance of these emotions is interpreted by the horse as punishment, as oppression, **because a horse does not experience such emotions**! He just employs methods of dominance with which he protects his personal space but, as with all he does, he does this reflexively not emotionally. So, if you are angry or in a bad mood with everything and anything, then even every well-intended aid, or even praise, becomes punishment.

2. It develops, as a rule, from a demand. For example, I want to go left but the horse wants to go right: he gets smacked in the head; I want to halt, the horse wants to keep going: I get angrier and angrier. All of this falls under my definition of punishment that arises out of my demand and which is absolutely forbidden. The only thing that helps in this kind of situation is the type of schooling depicted in this book and systematic progression.

3. Punishment is always in the cards when, as I describe it, the timing is not synchronized. For example, my stallion sees a beautiful mare behind me, a mare sweeter and lovelier than I can ever be. He forgets his good schooling, stamps angrily a couple of times, and begins to charge, intending to clear me, the obstacle to true love, out of his way. One gesture from me calls the out-of-control animal back to 'order' and I will ask him for five steps backwards to re-establish dominance. But if, prior to asking him to back, I have to sort out my lead line or pick up the whip that I dropped in shock because of his behaviour, then a few seconds pass before I can ask him to back the five steps. Because of this pause, he would interpret the subsequent backing as punishment for no reason, because he would no longer connect my action with his past misbehaviour but rather with the five seconds of standing still! In the eyes of the horse I am punishing him for absolutely correct behaviour.

Some of you will consider this nit-picking and that would be correct, but the sum of these 'nits' creates a bank of correct or incorrect behaviour, and yields, ultimately, either harmony or chaos. That is why it is so immensely important that it becomes part of your very being to constantly, consciously control yourself and always reflect upon your actions.

The protection of personal space

Let us stay with the above example. The stallion, blinded by love, charges at me, and, for whatever reason, does not respond to my signal to stop, he simply keeps running. What do I do? Very simple: **I hit him and very soundly**! That is why these definitions are coming at the end of the book, so that this instruction will be understood as I intend it to be and not taken out of context. In such a situation, where it is a matter of *your* personal space, your safety, you cannot be energetic enough. **But there are two critical, elementary things you absolutely must heed.**

If you have hit your horse in such a situation, he will immediately back off and if you now show anger or, what is worse, hit him again, then you will most probably ruin many weeks of work, you will fall back into the barbaric times of punishment. 'Punishment' is connected with emotion and being out of synchronization. Both of which have occurred here.

If your horse has backed-off after the first blow, then **refrain from any further angry behaviour**! Instead, do what I describe below.

I now want to share one of my little secrets with you. This often confuses people observing my work; they are not only confused by my behaviour, but also by the horse's response.

When I have to protect myself by striking my horse (as not infrequently happens) I not only do not get angry but, instead, I become very friendly in the same instant and immediately stroke the horse in the spot where I just hit him. When you do this you are behaving like a high-ranking animal, and the results are amazing. Your horse is not startled or made sour but now trustingly acknowledges your personal space and your dominance. You are, to your horse, a high-ranking being, whom he can understand and in whom he can trust.

This behaviour which I call **releasing**, is of immense importance. Self-discipline is demanded for this, because our behaviour in just such exceptional situations either strengthens our relationship with the horse or distances us from him.

The use of dominance tools/aids

The dominance tools define themselves very easily, because everything that does not fall into the first two categories belongs to the dominance aids, of which countless ones have been described in this book. But be careful; as has already been said, a dominance tool is a dominance tool only so long as it has none of the attributes of punishment. **Otherwise a useful tool becomes a destructive weapon.** The following is the most important dominance tool.

Backing-up as a dominance tool

Backing-up is sometimes rigorous and demanding for the horse, and therefore it is such an effective tool. Your horse has learned to step backwards from slight, subtle signals. If, now, he should begin to 'fight' you for some reason, it might show itself in the following ways.

- He mouths you – this is a major disregard of your dominance.
- He rubs himself on you to scratch an itch or rub off a fly – this, too, is a major disregard of your dominance. (This is intended particularly for you ladies. The above actions are anything but friendly, sympathetic, gestures: the horse is saying that you are about as important as a tree a pig scratches on. A horse is a horse, not a human, and a horse shows us his friendship and sympathy in very different ways.)
- He leaves his position when being led, pushes ahead, etc. Once again, he is disregarding your dominance.

In all these cases, and many others, a few steps of backing up will send the horse back to his subordinate position. You always do this with a friendly demeanor and affection while emphasizing your position. After three or four steps, halt him and praise generously your now-obedient horse.

Work becomes play

I would now like to shed light on another important question, namely: for how long should a horse be worked?

You really have to judge this by instinct and feel. I try to proceed so that the work becomes play and that the transition from 'normal life' to concentrated work is practically imperceptible to the horse. As a rule I confine really concentrated work with the horse to a few minutes. I am guided by my observations of the horse's response and my intuition: there are no hard and fast rules. I adhere to two important principles. If a horse has willingly and cheerfully attempted an exercise and performed it well and contentedly then I end the lesson. That could happen after as little as thirty seconds.

As I mentioned in the chapter on learning, it is not the length of the lesson that determines the success but the quality of the lesson, how well it has been understood and whether or not a specific learning goal has been achieved. There are two things relevant to this that I always try to keep distinctly separate from one another:

is the work being done at this moment about fitness or very specifically about education?

What do I mean by that? Lunge work, pole work, the first steps under saddle and all the exercises that were described in this book, serve to impart educational content to the horse and to supple him. None of these exercises is intended exclusively to condition him but these things are commonly lumped together. So, a horse is often chased around the arena for an hour or more in order to condition him and educate him at the same time. Consequently the horse gets bored and, after a short time, loses his concentration. He associates the arena with uncomfortable, boring work.

The picadero, the arena, the surveyor's-tape lane, i.e. the schoolroom, I use exclusively to **educate!** If the lesson content is understood after one minute, then the 'student' is praised and dismissed from class. For conditioning there are large fields, paddocks and the countryside in which horses should be put through their paces.

Riding-in young horses

To discuss this complex topic fully would require another book but the basic procedure is the same as has been described in this one.

It is critical that the work progresses step by step, and that the element of play remains in the foreground. Taking walks is the most important way to start a young horse's education. At the start, the picadero and the riding arena should only be used occasionally for a few minutes.

Trust, respect and fun in the work are

the first and most important lessons. After that, the youngster should be led round the countryside from an obedient and reliable horse. Then with his first gymnasticizing lunge work and the first careful lateral movements, the horse will become accustomed to his work joyfully and enthusiastically.

When he is used to walking round the countryside you can get on the young horse every once in a while so that he learns that carrying a rider is nothing to worry about.

If you ride-in a young horse naturally and in a spirit of play, rebellion and evasions do not crop up. During the daily walks I, now and then, hop up on the horse's back and, before we know it, the wild horse has become a riding horse.

As soon as he is accustomed to the saddle, he can be taken for more short trips into the countryside, again accompanied by a reliable companion horse. In this way a young horse grows into his role as a riding horse without any traumatic experiences.

Why are the reins there?

'Collected riding on a loose rein' was the theme of this book but the majority of the exercises have in fact been done without reins, and what exactly a loose rein is has not been discussed. A loose rein is, naturally, one that visibly loops. There are three distinct training phases in which these loose reins are used but these phases also cross over and complement each other.

In the first of these phases, the horse learns to move under the rider, to recognize and accept full and half-halts, all totally independently of the reins. The tasks for which the reins are usually employed are undertaken wholly by the body: body language, the displacement of body weight etc.

Once horse and rider have learned this, there follows a phase of training in which two of the *four* available reins are taken up so that, **subsequently, contact with the mouth as well as the nose could be taken**!

Even this rein is a loose rein, because it has no mechanical effect on the act of riding; the directing of the horse, all halts and half-halts and collecting aids continue to be undertaken by the body and independently of the reins.

Even at this stage the reins are not used to slow the horse, halt him, turn or collect him – all these things can be ridden just as well and just as precisely without them. Ultimately, the reins are used only to perfect the overall picture; they are used solely through the most subtle 'impulses', to provide the final polish to the complete harmony of two beings.

The third phase introduces the curb rein which can be held in one hand, again lightly and loosely. When a horse goes well in a curb, perfection is attained; the fine subtle play of the little finger with the weight of the reins has become another powerful signal.

Four reins, the bridle and bits

I hope by now it has become clear when reins are used and how they should be used.

Basically, reins are used to give signals from top to bottom. By that I mean that the impulse, the stimulus, is first applied to the nose, then to the snaffle, and lastly to the curb. To sensitize the horse to each level, moving from level to level, four reins are employed. The top ones are used in the way described above and the bottom ones carry over the same signal exclusively through the weight of the reins. By being worked through the levels, the horse is sensitized to, and learns to accept, the rein and bit contact.

In the transition from one type of bridling to another, all four reins are employed equally to give a signal so that in the transition from noseband to snaffle, snaffle to curb, and then to curb alone, the snaffle reins take on the role previously performed by the reins attached to the cavesson noseband.

The sequence is always as follows: ride-in the horse in the halter – without reins or bit. Then, slowly make the transition to a four-rein system as shown in the top photo (right). A soft headstall is – as described by Pluvinel, for example – combined with a snaffle bit so that the horse is worked with the reins attached to the snaffle hanging more loosely than those attached to the noseband.

The horse should now be taken out into the country in his new noseband/snaffle combination to ensure that he still responds well to our body language and can be ridden independently of the reins. When he shows the first beautiful signs of proud self-carriage and collection (hock flexion) in an elevated frame, then, finally, a dressage curb can be added and the snaffle reins now take over the duties formerly performed by the reins attached to the

Here we have the very handsome riding pony stallion Don Basilico from Klosterkielhof in three different bridles, each appropriate to one of the three stages of bridling and bitting. In the first photo we see a Hannoverian bridle which has been converted to a leather headstall. The reins are buckled to the noseband. At the beginning of the work the snaffle reins hang more loosely than those attached to the noseband.

In the second photo we see a simple curb bit added, which is to be used only as described above; you can break a horse's lower jaw with such a curb. One set of reins is attached to the snaffle, one set to the curb.

The third photo shows this handsome boy in a bit that is the epitome of riding. A rider who presents a horse bitted this way demonstrates that he has reached the peak of his craft and achieved the true art of riding.

cavesson noseband. The subtle signals at present being given to the snaffle now travel over the two curb reins to the curb bit, which, in the end remains the only and unbelievably tender connection to the horse's mouth.

Integration into daily life

The schooling programme described in this book puts very high, if not the highest, demands on the horseman. But, in the end, what do you do with that schooling?

It is wonderful to educate a horse in this way – to start at zero and to slowly become one with your horse. But how does this fit in with the reality of your everyday life? I would like to dedicate the last paragraphs of this book to your everyday life and your intuition.

When you go out into the countryside with your horse you will resort to taking up the reins and use them to turn your horse and to halt him, and that will, realistically, not be easy to change quickly. So, how do you proceed? In my courses I always illustrate this dilemma as follows.

When an experienced yogi teaches a student about the 'wonder world of true life' he, finally, after weeks have passed, says to his pupil, 'And now, continue exactly as you have done up until now! The large plant that represents the dark side of your life has grown into a powerful tree. If you now try to tear it up by the roots it will cost you infinite amounts of strength and all you will have to show for your efforts is a large, painful hole. The path of the wise man is a different one. He sows the seeds of good in himself without acknowledging the shadow cast by the tree of evil. His interest and his love are for the new. This is what he will nourish and care for. And so the seed will grow, and more and more it will take the light from the tree of evil. So, you will make a gradual transition which costs you no useless expenditure of power and is, above all, a guarantee of success'.

And that is exactly what you should do too! Continue doing exactly as you have done up to now. Let these new ideas ripen within you and slowly begin to incorporate this new way of thinking into your daily practice. Start with the leading work, with the work in the picadero, experiment with riding more and more independently of the reins, and continue to develop your body language.

Think about ambition, which we want to cast aside, and think about the time remaining to you and your horse. Nurture the seeds of the new and nourish them!

The old fisherman and intuition

In the south of the land where the western world sinks into the Atlantic, so goes the tale, a small group of knights and fishermen lived peacefully alongside one another. The knights' castle was ruled by a wise man, whom no one really saw or knew. One day this man heard of a wise old fisherman who always had the richest catches of anyone in the village. The knight learned that this old fisherman intended to point out exactly all the richest fishing grounds on a large map. So, the knight saddled his horse and made his way into the village. When he found the fisherman he questioned him about his intention: 'Why do you want to do this? Whom do you want to serve?'

'Oh worthy knight, I am an old man, and before I die I want to pass my knowledge on to the living.'

'To what do you owe your knowledge?' asked the knight.

'Well,' said the fisherman, 'I owe it to my good nose, to my rich and vast experience and, above all, to my intuition'.

'So, why do you want to rob the young men of the village of the chance to develop a good nose, rich experience and, above all, their own good intuition?'

The old fisherman turned away without a word, smiling. Today, on his gravestone one can still read: 'I took my knowledge with me to the grave, but I leave you Intuition'.

In this spirit,
Klaus Ferdinand Hempfling
Vilanova, Spain
January, 1993